NUTRITION
FOR
CYCLISTS

NUTRITION
FOR
CYCLISTS

JANE GRIFFIN

THE CROWOOD PRESS

First published in 2014 by
The Crowood Press Ltd
Ramsbury, Marlborough
Wiltshire SN8 2HR

www.crowood.com

British Library Cataloguing-in-Publication Data
A catalogue record for this book is available from the British Library.

ISBN 978 1 84797 842 4

Acknowledgements
To my husband Chris for his love, support, encouragement and wise words – not to mention the endless mugs of tea and coffee and the evening meals he produced while I shut myself away in my study.

A very big thank-you must go to Nigel Mitchell, the Head of Nutrition at British Cycling/Team Sky. On a trip to the Velodrome in Manchester, we sat watching the top cyclists in the country train as Nigel told me about the Tour de France and the nutritional requirements generally of elite cyclists, both in training and in races.

Another thank-you goes to the Dairy Council for giving me permission to reproduce the diet plan which appeared in their publication *Nutrition for Cyclists – the Milk Race*.

Typeset by Servis Filmsetting Ltd, Stockport, Cheshire

Printed and bound in India by Replika Press Pvt Ltd

CONTENTS

INTRODUCTION

In the 2014 Annual Report of the Chief Medical Officer, Professor Dame Sally Davies said that while many people think cycling is dangerous because we hear about deaths on the road, cycling is usually a safe and healthy thing to do but the benefits don't make the headlines. The *British Medical Journal* published an article in February 2014 entitled 'London bike hire has positive impact on health'. The researchers from the medical school in Cambridge investigated to see if the physical activity of cycling outweighed the risks of road traffic accidents, collisions and inhalation of polluted air. The results showed the greatest benefit was to older users (over 29) and particularly to men but also women.

Cycling, rather like running, is a simple sport! A runner needs a pair of decent running shoes and a water bottle; a cyclist needs a bike and a water bottle. Those are the basics; of course there can be many more 'add-ons', such as special clothing, shoes and gadgets, but it is not a complicated sport. A cyclist can go out alone, or with the family, or cycle with a friend, a neighbour or a cycling club. A cyclist can go out for a long ride or just a short ride.

As a sport, cycling has blossomed in recent years, no doubt in part because of the success of British Cycling at events such as the Olympics and the Tour de France. Long may this enthusiasm for cycling continue!

CHAPTER 1

NUTRITION BASICS

Cyclists rely on what they eat and drink every day to supply all their energy and nutrient requirements. The one exception to this is vitamin D, which the body can make by the action of sunlight on bare skin. The need for a special diet is therefore very small for most people and cyclists who go out on their bikes regularly should certainly be making sufficient vitamin D – as long as enough skin is exposed! So what does the diet have to provide to keep the cycling body fit, healthy and stored with enough energy to meet each day's requirements?

The body needs a regular supply of water, energy (calories), carbohydrate, fat and protein, vitamins and minerals. Requirements for health and well-being can easily be met by a varied diet – in other words, one that contains lots of different foods and drinks. For most people, problems arise not so much because of a scarcity of food (as happens in times of famine through crop failure or over-population) but rather through intakes that are habitually greater than requirements. An advantage of taking part in regular exercise such as cycling means that cyclists need to eat and enjoy more food than sedentary individuals, while still being able to maintain a healthy weight for their sport. However, this does not mean they have an open invitation to eat anything (fast foods, for example) or to eat as much as possible at every meal. Achieving the right quality, quantity and variety of food and fluids consumed on a daily basis is the nutritional key to remaining healthy and maximizing cycling performance. Too little and the body could be likened to a car with an empty petrol tank: in other words, it's not going anywhere very fast! Regularly consuming more than the body needs leads to an increase in body-weight (as body fat) and a much greater effort will be required to maintain cycling intensity and/or duration. If daily food choices do not meet daily requirements for energy and nutrients, performance will suffer, the risk of infections and injuries will increase, and there may even be long-term health implications. Not only do nutrients have different functions in the body, but the type and quantity of nutrients in what we eat varies from food to food. Understanding what energy and nutrients do in the body, and which foods are good sources of particular nutrients, provides the foundations to build the best possible diet to maximize performance both in training and races. Not only that, it will help in keeping the body fit and healthy. On the practical side, the diet must fit into a cyclist's lifestyle and daily schedule – and just as importantly it must be enjoyable. It can be very hard for a cyclist to meet the increased energy and nutrient requirements of cycling when training hard and regularly, especially on top of holding down a job or studying and having some social and family life too. This can be particularly difficult if food consumed on a daily basis is boring and repetitive, and may not be what the body needs nutritionally in terms of quality and quantity.

Nutrients and their main functions

Food is made up of carbohydrate, fat, protein, vitamins, minerals and water. In some foods, particularly fruit and vegetables, a very large proportion is water, whereas in others, such as oils and fats, the water content is minimal. The amounts and indeed the presence of the different vitamins and minerals can vary considerably between foods, too. Health professionals spend a lot of time encouraging people to eat a diet that contains a wide variety of different foods to help ensure that the requirements for all the essential nutrients are being met on a regular basis. Carbohydrate and fat are the major sources of energy or fuel for the human body. Protein, however, has a unique function. It provides the material for growth and repair of the body. Vitamins and minerals are essential nutrients and the body depends on the diet to supply them, with the exception of vitamin D, which can be made by the action of sunlight on the skin (as already mentioned). However, in some parts of the world the amount of daily sunlight can be very limited, with a risk that some people living in these places might become vitamin D deficient. The vast majority of vitamins and minerals are needed in very small amounts, yet they have vital and very varied roles to play in maintaining health and well-being. Vitamins make up quite a diverse group of substances that are important in the regulation of different chemical processes constantly going on in the body. They are not a source of energy, though many vitamins are involved in the release of energy from food. Minerals, rather like vitamins, also have many different functions. They help in controlling the composition of bodily fluids and are important constituents of teeth and bones. They are also essential components of enzymes, which act like biological catalysts regulating biochemical reactions, and also of proteins, such as the oxygen-carrying haemoglobin.

Energy

The energy needed by the body comes solely from the diet – in other words, the food and fluids we consume on a regular, daily basis. Our bodies digest, absorb and metabolize what we eat and drink, releasing energy for the body to use. As the body's energy requirements increase, more food and fluids will need to be consumed to meet these requirements. Active individuals will therefore have greater requirements than sedentary individuals (in some cases considerably greater). Taking part in a sport such as cycling not only helps the body keep healthy, but also means that cyclists are able to enjoy their food without constantly worrying about eating more than their body needs with the inevitable gain in weight. However, it is not an invitation to eat to excess or 'fit to bursting'!

The energy value of food

1g protein → 4kcals

1g fat → 9kcals

1g carbohydrate → 3.75kcals (on food labels a factor of 4kcal is used)

1g alcohol → 7kcals

1g water → 0kcals

These nutrients make up most of the weight of a food. Vitamins and minerals, though vitally important in the diet, account for very little of the actual weight of the food. Fruit and vegetables contain a large percentage of water and as a result have relatively fewer calories than fatty foods such as butter, margarine, lard and oils, which all have a low water content and therefore a much higher calorie count on a weight basis. It is worth mentioning

here that water does not have a calorie value – it really does contain no calories, whether it is out of a tap or out of a bottle! The vast majority of foods are a mixture of nutrients and the energy value of any particular food will be the sum of the energy value of each nutrient (carbohydrate, fat, protein and alcohol).

Carbohydrate

Carbohydrates are found in the diet either as simple carbohydrates (sugars) or as starches. Most dietary carbohydrate is plant in origin. The only exception is lactose, the sugar that occurs in milk whether it is from a human, cow, goat or other mammal. Fruits and fruit juices, milk and milk products, honey and sugar are the main sources of simple carbohydrates in our diet. They can be identified easily by their sweet taste. Simple carbohydrates have often been vilified. The famous nutritionist Professor John Yudkin wrote a book, first published in 1972, entitled *Pure, White and Deadly*. He was one of the first scientists to claim that sugar was a major cause of obesity and heart disease. (He was also this author's professor of nutrition at London University.) Apart from sugar, there are many other factors that need to be considered when determining the causes of these health problems, including intakes of fat, saturated fat, salt and alcohol, inactivity and smoking. It is not the purpose of this book to debate this topic but it is perhaps pertinent to remember that sugar grows naturally as sugar cane and sugar beet and that it also occurs naturally in fruits and certain root vegetables, including carrots. Sugar (or sucrose, to give the correct terminology) is made up of two simple sugars, glucose and fructose. There is no nutritional difference between white and brown sugar. It is all a matter of taste and appearance. Simple carbohydrates are all characterized by their sweet taste. Starchy or complex carbohydrates are found in bread, pasta, rice, potatoes, breakfast cereals, pulses and sweetcorn.

Carbohydrates are the most important source of energy in the diet as they are the optimum energy source for exercising muscles, the brain and the central nervous system. Anyone who has tried to follow the one-time popular low-carbohydrate/high-protein diet will surely remember how tired, lethargic and irritable they were as their body became more and more carbohydrate depleted. The amount of carbohydrate that our bodies can store in the liver and muscles (known as liver or muscle glycogen) is limited. This helps to explain why sports dietitians and sports nutritionists put so much emphasis on foods that provide carbohydrate. (*See* Chapter 3 for sources of carbohydrate.)

Dietary Fibre

Fibre was originally called roughage, which, according to the author's dictionary, is 'the coarse indigestible constituents of food which provide bulk to the diet and aid digestion'. It is now called non-starch polysaccharide (NSP) but most people still refer to it as dietary fibre, which is also the terminology or wording used on food labels. Fibre is a major component of plant cell walls. The key dietary contributors of fibre are therefore fruits, vegetables and cereals. Dietary fibre can be soluble or insoluble, and it is the solubility or lack of it that determines its function. People are encouraged to eat more insoluble fibre because of its ability to help keep the lower part of the digestive system (the bowels) functioning in a healthy and regular manner. It does this by absorbing water, which makes the gut contents heavier, which in turn speeds up the movement down the gut. This can help in relieving constipation and other bowel disorders. The main contributors of insoluble fibre in the diet are cereals such as wheat, maize and rice.

Soluble fibre occurs particularly in oats, legumes (peas and beans), leafy vegetables and some fruits, most notably apples. It has quite different effects in the body from insoluble fibre, probably playing a part in helping to lower blood cholesterol levels and slow down the rate of post-prandial absorption of glucose (particularly important in some types of diabetes). Healthy eating messages encourage the inclusion of dietary fibre in the diet of the general population. As carbohydrate figures strongly in the dietary recommendations for cyclists, it is likely that the vast majority of cyclists consume sufficient dietary fibre without the need to choose high-fibre sources. Cyclists who actually prefer high-fibre foods from an organoleptic point of view (i.e. they like the taste/texture better), will need to be careful about how much high-fibre food they consume on a regular basis and should certainly take particular care not to overload with high-fibre foods on race days! (*See* Chapter 9 for the reasons why.)

Fat

Fat is an essential nutrient and an important source of energy. Many people eat excessive amounts of high-fat foods and would benefit from reducing their intake. However, fat should never be avoided totally. Apart from supplying the body with energy, fat also supplies the essential fatty acids of the omega-3 and omega-6 families. These are termed 'essential' because the human body is unable to make them and must rely on supplies provided by the diet. Other functions performed by fat include insulating and protecting the internal organs in the body, acting as carriers for fat soluble vitamins and antioxidants, and playing a part in the formation of certain hormones. Hormones are chemicals that are made in one part of the body and have an effect in another part of the body. They act as chemical messengers

to regulate specific body functions. For example, insulin is a hormone made in the pancreas, specifically in the beta cells of the Islets of Langerhans (remember that for a quiz supper question!), but it has the job of controlling the concentration of glucose in the blood.

Fat plays another important part, particularly in the enjoyment of what we eat. Many flavours, smells and textures are linked to the fats in food and without them our food would taste remarkably bland. It may make our food more enjoyable, but an excessive amount of fat in the diet is not to be recommended as it is considered to be one of the risk factors linked to the development of chronic diseases, particularly obesity and heart disease. Reducing fat intake is not necessarily a simple thing to achieve as the amount of fat in food is not always obvious to the consumer; some is very visible, such as butter and margarine, while some is hidden, as in eggs and homogenized milk.

Protein

Protein performs vital structural functions in the body and can be found in muscle, bone, cartilage, tendons, ligaments, skin and hair. It is needed for growth and development, and has an on-going role in rebuilding, repairing and maintaining vital body tissues. Enzymes are proteins that can act as catalysts, increasing the velocity or

Poultry is a good source of protein, but the skin is also a source of fat.

Sources of fat

Visible fat:

Butter, margarine, ghee

Oils, lard, suet, dripping

Hydrogenated fats and vegetable shortening

Cream

Fat on meat, poultry skin

Oily fish

Invisible fat:

Very lean cuts of meat

Cheese

Whole milk (full fat)

– Semi-skimmed milk

– Skimmed milk

Eggs

Meat products: pies, pasties, sausages, burgers, pâté, salami, tinned meats

Chips, crisps and roast potatoes

Nuts, olives, avocado pears

Fried food and pastry

Some cakes and biscuits

Creamy puddings and cheesecake

Mayonnaise, salad cream, creamy sauces

Peanut butter

Chocolate, toffee and fudge

Eggs have a high protein content and high biological value.

speed of biochemical reactions taking place in the body. Some hormones are proteinous in nature. Insulin, which is responsible for preventing excessive rises in blood glucose levels, is an example of a proteinous hormone. Other proteins have important roles to play in the immune system, where they help to fight off infections, while others act as transporters of fats, minerals and oxygen. In some situations protein can be used as a source of energy, but with so many unique functions this is usually a last resort. Protein, unlike fat (and to a certain extent carbohydrate), cannot be stored in the body. If more protein is eaten than is needed, part of the protein molecule is broken down and excreted from the body in urine and the rest is used as an immediate source of energy or it can be converted into fat and stored.

Amino Acids

Amino acids are the building blocks of protein, and all the various proteins needed by the human body can be made from just twenty different amino acids. Essential amino acids cannot be made by

Sources of protein

Animal sources:

Meat

Offal (kidney, liver, heart, tongue, tripe)

Poultry

Fish (white, oily and shellfish)

Eggs

Milk, cheese, yoghurt

Vegetable sources:

Beans, peas and lentils

Nuts and seeds

Quorn and tofu

Soya beans, soya milk

Textured vegetable protein

Bread, potatoes, rice, pasta, cereals

Classification of amino acids

Essential amino acids:

Histidine (only in infants)

Isoleucine

Leucine

Lysine

Methionine

Phenylalanine

Threonine

Tryptophan

Valine

Non-essential amino acids:

Alanine

Arginine

Asparagine

Aspartic acid

Cysteine/cystine

Glutamic acid

Glutamine

Glycine

Proline

Serine

Tyrosine

the body and must therefore be supplied by the diet. Non-essential amino acids can be made from other amino acids.

Animal protein versus vegetable protein

The amount of protein in a particular food is obviously important, particularly when a cyclist is aiming for a specific protein intake. However, the quality of the protein must also be taken into account, so it is important to have some knowledge about which amino acids are present in a protein and in what amounts, as well as the overall quantity of protein. Animal sources of protein such as meat, fish, eggs, milk and cheese have high protein contents with a high biological value. Pulses (soya bean, kidney beans, chickpeas, lentils and peanuts) have very

high protein contents and a high (in the case of soya) or medium biological value. Beans and peas belong to a food group called legumes; contrary to popular belief, peanuts fall into this category too. Peanuts grow underground and hence are also called ground nuts. Cereals (wheat, rice, barley, maize and oats) have medium protein contents and, with one exception, a low biological value; the exception is rice, which has a medium value. Nuts (walnuts, brazil nuts, hazelnuts, cashews,

Opt for wholemeal bread where possible as it is a good source of the B complex vitamins.

almonds, pine nuts and pistachios) have high protein contents but their biological value is on the low side. Starchy roots (potato, cassava, yam and sweet potato) are low in protein and also have a low or negligible biological value. Vegetables and fruits are low in protein; in fact they are not really thought of as a source of protein – they have far more important roles to play in the daily diet.

Excessive protein intakes

A diet that regularly contains unnecessarily high amounts of protein will place an increased workload on the kidneys as they have to excrete what the body does not need. In healthy people this may not present any problems, but it may do for some cyclists, particularly those who are not very good at replacing fluid lost through sweating (*see* Chapter 4).

Vitamins

Vitamins are complex organic substances that are needed in very small amounts but nevertheless have vital and quite varied functions in the body. With the exception of vitamin D, which can be made by the action of sunlight (UV light) on exposed skin, the diet must provide all these vitamins. Vitamin deficiencies are rare in the UK although they still occur in some parts of the world where diets are very limited, either because of severe shortages of food or through a lack of variety in the diet. Vitamins A, D, E and K are fat-soluble vitamins that can be stored in the body. Vitamin C and the B complex vitamins are water soluble and are not stored in the body. Water soluble vitamins consumed in excess of the body's requirements are usually excreted by the kidneys in the urine.

Vitamin A
Major food sources:
Vitamin A is found in animal foods as retinol. Plant foods contain beta-carotene, the precursor of vitamin A. The richest sources of vitamin A are fish liver oils (cod liver oil) and animal liver (lamb, calf and pig). Good sources of vitamin A include oily fish (mackerel, herring, tuna, sardines and salmon), egg yolks, full fat milk, butter, cheese and fortified margarine. Good sources of beta-carotene are fruit and vegetables, especially orange ones (carrots, apricots), dark green ones (spinach, watercress and broccoli) and red ones (tomatoes and red peppers).

Main functions:
Essential for healthy skin.
Maintains healthy mucous membranes in the throat and nose.
Protects against poor vision in dim light.
Antioxidant properties.

Deficiency:
Very rare in the UK but in Third World Countries vitamin A deficiency is a major cause of blindness.

Requirements:
Reference Nutrient Intake (RNI) for adult women is 600µg per day and for adult men is 700µg per day.

Excessive intake:
Regular intake of retinol should not exceed 7,500µg for adult women, 9,000µg for adult men and 3,300µg for pregnant women. Women who are or might become pregnant are advised by the Department of Health not to take vitamin A supplements or eat liver, as excessive amounts can be toxic and dangerous to the unborn child.

Vitamin B₁ (thiamin)
Major food sources:
Cereal products such as breakfast cereals, bread, pasta and rice, lean pork and peas, beans and lentils.

Main functions:
Release of energy from carbohydrate.
For normal functioning of nerves, brain
and muscles.

Deficiency:
Very rare in the UK but causes beri-
beri, which affects the heart and nervous
system.

Requirements:
RNI is 1.0mg per day for adult men
and 0.8mg per day for adult women.
(Dependent on the energy content of
the diet, an RNI is set at 0.4mg per
1,000kcals for most groups of people.)

Excessive intake:
Chronic intake in excess of 3g per day is
toxic in adults.

Vitamin B₂ (riboflavin)
Major food sources:
Milk, egg yolks, liver, kidneys, cheese,
wholemeal bread and cereals, green
vegetables. Sensitive to light.

Main functions:
Release of energy from carbohydrate, fat
and protein.

Deficiency:
Severe deficiency is unlikely in UK but
causes sores in the corners of the mouth.

Requirements:
RNI for adult men is 1.3mg per day and
for adult women 1.1mg per day.

Excessive intake:
Absorption of riboflavin in the intestine is
limited so toxic effects are unlikely.

*Niacin (nicotinic acid, nicotinamide,
vitamin B₃)*
Major food sources:
Meat, poultry, fortified breakfast cereals,
white flour and bread, yeast extracts.

Main functions:
Release of energy from protein, fat and
carbohydrate.

Deficiency:
Rare.

Requirements:
RNI for adult men is 17mg per day and
for adult women 13mg per day.

Excessive intake:
Very high intake in the region of 3–6g per
day may cause liver damage.

Vitamin B₆ (pyridoxine)
Major food sources:
Meat, particularly beef and poultry, fish,
wholemeal bread and fortified breakfast
cereals.

Main functions:
Needed for protein metabolism, central
nervous system functioning, haemoglobin
production and antibody formation.

Deficiency:
Deficiency signs are rare.

Requirements:
RNI for adult men is 1.4mg per day and for adult women 1.2mg per day.

Excessive intake:
High intake has been associated with impaired function of sensory nerves. The amounts involved have varied from 50mg per day to 2–7g per day.

Vitamin B₁₂ (cyanocobalamin)

Major food sources:
Found only in food of animal origin (liver, kidney, meat, oily fish, milk, cheese and eggs). Some breakfast cereals are fortified with vitamin B_{12} Some vegetarian foods are also fortified, for example soya protein, soya milks, yeast extract.

Main functions:
Red blood cell formation, maintenance of nervous system and protein metabolism.

Deficiency:
Pernicious anaemia (blood disorder).

Requirements:
RNI for adult men and women is 1.5µg per day.

Excessive intake:
Excess is excreted in the urine and therefore is not dangerous.

Folic acid (folates)

Major food sources:
Liver, kidney, green leafy vegetables, wholegrain cereals, fortified breakfast cereals and breads, eggs, pulses, bananas and orange juice.

Main functions:
Red and white blood cell formation in bone marrow.
Essential for growth.
Protection against neural tube defects (spina bifida) pre-conceptually and in early pregnancy.

Deficiency:
Megaloblastic anaemia (blood disorder).

Requirements:
RNI for adults is 200µg per day. Women who might become pregnant and women during the first twelve weeks of pregnancy are recommended to take an extra 400µg per day.

Excessive intake:
Dangers of toxicity are very low.

Biotin and Pantothenic acid

Major food sources:
Widespread in food.

Main functions:
Release of energy from fats, carbohydrates and protein.

Deficiency:
Unlikely.

Requirements:
None set.

Excessive intake:
No danger.

Vitamin C
Major food sources:
Fruit and vegetables, especially blackcurrants, strawberries and citrus fruit, raw peppers, tomatoes and green leafy vegetables, and potatoes because of the amount eaten.

Main functions:
For healthy skin, blood vessels, gums and teeth, wound healing, iron absorption and formation of antibodies. It is an important antioxidant.

Deficiency:
Serious deficiency causes scurvy. Mild deficiency leads to tiredness, bleeding gums, delayed wound healing and lowered resistance to infection.

Requirements:
RNI for adults is 40mg per day.

Excessive intake:
Intakes at levels of twenty times the RNI or more have been associated with diarrhoea and increased risk of oxalate stones in the kidney.

Vitamin D (cholecalciferol)
Major food sources:
Fortified margarines and spreads, fortified breakfast cereals, oily fish, egg yolks, full fat milk and dairy products. The main source of vitamin D is the action of sunlight (UV light) on the skin.

Main function:
Absorption of calcium and its utilization in the body, particularly the mineralization of bones and teeth.

Deficiency:
Loss of calcium from the bones causes rickets in young children and osteomalacia, particularly in women of child-bearing age.

Requirements:
No dietary source is needed for adults provided that their skin is exposed to sunlight (RNI for adults aged 65 and over is 10µg per day).

Excessive intake:
Toxicity is rare in adults.

Vitamin E
Major food sources:
Vegetable oils, seeds, nuts (especially peanuts), wheat germ, wholemeal bread and cereals, green plants, milk and milk products, and egg yolks.

Main functions:
Powerful antioxidant, protecting body tissues against free radical damage.

Deficiency:
None except in very exceptional circumstances.

Requirements:
No RNI set; 4mg per day for adult men and 3mg per day for adult women considered adequate.

Excessive intake:
Toxicity extremely rare.

Vitamin K
Major food sources:
Dark green leafy vegetables, margarines and vegetable oils, milk and liver. Vitamin K can also be synthesized by bacteria in the gut.

Main functions:
Blood clotting.

Deficiency:
Rare in adults.

Requirements:
No RNI set, but 1µg per kg per day is considered both safe and adequate.

Excessive intake:
Natural K vitamins seem free from toxic side-effects, even at up to a hundred times the safe intake. Synthetic forms may not have such a wide margin of safety.

Minerals

Minerals are organic substances that the body needs to perform a variety of different and vital functions. Certain minerals are needed to build and maintain strong bones and teeth. Others are required to transport oxygen around the body, regulate water and acid-balance in the body, and activate and form essential parts of enzymes and hormones. Some are involved in fighting off infection; others help to maintain healthy levels of haemoglobin in the blood, release energy from food and transmit nerve impulses. Key to cyclists, some are vital in the relaxation and contraction of muscles. Most minerals must be supplied by the diet on a regular (daily) basis but also in the correct amounts – neither too much nor too little.

Calcium
Major food sources:
Milk, cheese and yoghurt (low-fat and full fat), tinned sardines and pilchards (from the edible bones), dark green leafy vegetables, pulses (including baked beans), white flour and white bread (fortified) and hard water.

Main functions:
Essential for strong and healthy bones and teeth. Important in blood clotting. Essential for nerve and muscle function.

Deficiency:
Causes problems with bones, which may become brittle and break easily (osteoporosis or brittle bone disease). Good calcium intakes in childhood and adolescence are vital to help build up calcium in the bones and to protect against osteoporosis in later life.

Requirements:
RNI for adult men and women is 700mg per day. Vitamin D is essential for the absorption of calcium.

Excessive intake:
Calcium toxicity is virtually unknown. The body adapts to high intakes by reducing the amount that is absorbed.

Phosphorus
Major food sources:
Present in all plant and animal foods except fats and sugars.

Main functions:
Essential for the formation of bones and teeth. Involved in many metabolic reactions.

Deficiency:
Unknown.

Requirements:
RNI for adult men and women is 550mg per day.

Excessive intake:
Not known in adults.

Magnesium
Major food sources:
Present in most foods, particularly cereals, vegetables (especially dark green leafy ones) and fruit.

Main functions:
Energy production, nerve and muscle function and bone structure.

Deficiency:
The body is very efficient at regulating magnesium content so deficiencies are rare. Usually caused by severe diarrhoea or excessive losses in the urine resulting from the use of diuretics.

Requirements:
RNI for adult men is 300mg per day and for adult women 270mg per day.

Excessive intake:
There is no evidence that high intakes are harmful if kidney function is normal.

Sodium and chloride
Major food sources:
As sodium chloride, better known as table salt. About 15–20 per cent of dietary sodium chloride is naturally present in food, 15–29 per cent is added in cooking or to the food once served and 60–79 per cent is added during food processing or manufacture. Foods high in sodium chloride include ham, bacon, smoked fish, foods canned in brine, cheese, salted butter, salted nuts and biscuits and yeast extract. Significant contributions to intake are also made because of the quantities of bread, breakfast cereal, ready meats, canned meats, savoury snacks, soups and sauces consumed on a regular basis.

Main functions:
Regulation of body water content, maintenance of acid-base balance, blood volume and blood pressure, and nerve and muscle function.

Deficiency:
Unlikely in normal circumstances.

Requirements:
RNI for adult men and women is 1,600mg per day for sodium and 2,500mg per day for chloride. The Food Standards Agency and UK Health Departments advise intake to be kept at or below 6g salt a day.

Excessive intake:
There is good evidence for a direct association between salt intake and high blood pressure.

Potassium

Major food sources:
Present in all foods except fats, oils and sugar. Particularly good sources are fruits (bananas and oranges), vegetables, potatoes, coffee, tea and cocoa.

Main functions:
Regulation of fluid balance in conjunction with sodium. Potassium maintains water inside the cells (intracellular fluid) and sodium maintains water outside the cells (extracellular fluid). Appears to have a positive effect in reducing blood pressure – a good reason to maintain fruit and vegetable intakes. Involved in nerve and muscle function.

Deficiency:
Unlikely but it can result from severe diarrhoea and vomiting.

Requirements:
RNI for adult men and women is 3,500mg per day.

Excessive intake:
Toxicity is only likely to occur through inappropriate supplementation.

Iron

Major food sources:
Liver, lean meat (especially red meat), kidney, heart, shellfish and egg yolks. Also wholegrain cereals, dried pulses and dried fruit, but it is less well absorbed than iron from animal foods. Some breakfast cereals are fortified with iron. Vitamin C helps the absorption of iron from plant foods.

Main function:
Part of haemoglobin in red blood cells which carries oxygen to all parts of the body.

Deficiency:
Low haemoglobin levels cause tiredness and fatigue and ultimately iron deficiency anaemia. As many as one in three women of child-bearing age in the UK is iron deficient.

Requirements:
RNI for women (11–50+ years) is 14.8mg per day. RNI for adult men is 8.7mg per day. (The RNI for women is higher to make up for iron losses due to menstruation.)

Excessive intake:
No risk from normal foods other than in people with rare metabolic disorders.

Zinc
Major food sources:
Red meat, liver, shellfish (especially oysters), dairy products and eggs. Wholegrain cereals, bread and pulses contain zinc, but it is less well-absorbed than zinc from animal sources.

Main functions:
Part of many enzymes needed for a variety of body functions. Involved in energy production, aiding wound healing, development of the body's immune system (antioxidant function) and insulin production.

Deficiency:
Insufficient zinc can slow down growth and development. It also delays wound healing and may impair immune function.

Requirements:
RNI for adult men is 9.5mg per day and for adult women 7mg per day.

Excessive intake:
Acute ingestion of 2g of zinc produces nausea and vomiting. Long-term intake of 50mg per day interferes with copper metabolism.

Copper
Major food sources:
The best food sources include liver, shellfish, legumes, nuts and prunes. It is also found in meat, bread, cereals, green vegetables and cocoa beans (and therefore chocolate!).

Main functions:
Part of several enzyme systems, particularly those involved in metabolism and antioxidant functioning. Helps to protect against infections and may be helpful in protecting against cancer and heart disease.

Deficiency:
Rare in the UK except in genetic disorders or severe malnutrition.

Requirements:
RNI for adult men and women is 1.2mg per day.

Excessive intake:
High intake is toxic but only occurs in abnormal circumstances, such as contaminated water.

Selenium
Major food sources:
Wholegrain cereals, poultry, fish and shellfish, milk, egg yolks, brazil nuts, onions, garlic and mushrooms. The selenium content of food depends on the amount in the soil.

Main function:
Powerful antioxidant (protects cell membranes from oxidative damage).

Deficiency:
No clinical condition is associated with a dietary deficiency but there is a possible link with the development of heart disease.

Requirements:
RNI for adult men is 75µg per day and for adult women 60µg per day.

Excessive intake:
High levels (in excess of 1mg) are known to be toxic and an upper limit of 6µg per kg per day for adults has been set.

Fluoride
Major food sources:
Drinking water with high natural or added fluoride levels, fluoride toothpaste, fish and tea.

Main functions:
Bone and tooth mineralization and helping in the prevention of tooth decay.

Deficiency:
Increased susceptibility to tooth decay and lack of bone strength.

Requirements:
No RNI set.

Excessive intake:
Causes mottling of teeth.

Iodine
Major food sources:
The only natural rich source is seafood. Other sources are milk and milk products, kelp and vegetables grown in iodine-rich soils, and iodized salt.

Main function:
Functioning of the thyroid and formation of thyroid hormones.

Deficiency:
Resulting deficiency of thyroid hormone leads to a low metabolic rate and lethargy.

Requirements:
RNI for adult men and women is 140µg per day.

Excessive intake:
Not usually a problem.

Manganese
Major food sources:
Tea. Also found in nuts, legumes, bran, leafy green vegetables, whole grains and egg yolks.

Main functions:
Component of many enzymes involved in metabolism; necessary for bone and tendon formation.

Deficiency:
Unobserved except in experimental studies.

Requirements:
No RNI set but safe intakes are believed to be 1.4mg per day for adults.

Excessive intake:
One of the least toxic elements. Excess intakes are quickly excreted.

Chromium
Major food sources:
Meat, wholegrain cereals, legumes, nuts and Brewer's yeast.

Main functions:
Formation of insulin and lipoprotein metabolism.

Deficiency:
Unlikely on a normal mixed diet.

Requirements:
No RNI set but safe intake believed to be 25µg per day for adults.

Molybdenum
Major food sources:
Trace amounts found in many foods.

Main functions:
Occurs in enzymes involved in metabolism. Involved in storage of iron in the body.

Deficiency:
Reported on very low intakes (25µg per day) where the typical UK diet provides a mean of 128µg per day. Deficiency therefore rarely occurs.

Requirements:
No RNI set but safe intake is believed to lie between 50 and 400µg per day.

Sulphur
Sulphur is an essential nutrient but as it is found in all proteins, in fats and many body fluids, no Reference Nutrient Intake is set for it. If a cyclist is getting enough protein from their diet, they will also be getting enough sulphur. A deficiency of sulphur is very rare.

Antioxidant nutrients and free radicals

The antioxidant nutrients are vitamins A, C and E. The key minerals with antioxidant properties are zinc, iron, copper and selenium. Many fruits and vegetables contain phytochemicals (chemicals from plants), which also have potentially health-giving benefits. This partly explains the healthy eating message to 'eat at least five portions of fruit and vegetables' a day. When oxygen is used in chemical reactions within the body, harmful chemicals called free radicals are produced. These free radicals are unstable as part of their structure is missing and they attempt to make up the loss by stealing from other molecules. This can lead to tissue damage, which may eventually cause heart disease or some forms of cancer. Thankfully antioxidants can neutralize free radicals.

The five food groups

Bread, other cereals and potatoes:
Bread, potatoes, pasta and noodles, rice, breakfast cereals. Other cereal grains such as oats, maize, millet and cornmeal, and other starchy vegetables like yams and plantains. Beans, peas and lentils can be included in this group too.

Provide carbohydrate, dietary fibre, some calcium and iron, B vitamins. Predominantly low in fat.

Recommended to make these the main part of the diet.

Fruit and vegetables:
Fresh, frozen or canned fruit and vegetables and salad vegetables. Dried fruit and fruit juice can make up some of the choices.

Provide vitamins, particularly C, beta-carotene and folic acid, other antioxidants, dietary fibre and some carbohydrate. The darker the vegetables (broccoli, spinach, greens and peppers), the more beta-carotene is present. Fruit juice counts as only one portion, however much is drunk in a day. Beans and pulses can be eaten as part of this group but only count as one portion, however much is eaten in a day.

Recommended to eat at least five portions a day.

Milk and dairy foods:
Milk, cheese, yoghurt and fromage frais. This group does not include butter, eggs and cream.

Provides protein, calcium, vitamin B_{12}, and vitamins A and D (lower fat versions contain less of these fat-soluble vitamins).

Eat or drink in moderate amounts and choose lower fat versions whenever possible.

Meat, fish and alternatives:
Meat, poultry, fish, eggs, nuts, beans, peas and lentils. Includes bacon, salami and meat products such as sausages, beefburgers and pâté. Includes frozen and canned fish such as fishfingers, fish cakes, tuna and sardines.

Provides protein, iron, B vitamins, especially B_{12}, zinc and magnesium.

Beans, peas and lentils also provide dietary fibre.

Eat moderate amounts and choose lower fat versions whenever possible.

Foods containing fat; foods and drinks containing sugar:
Fat:
Margarine, butter and other spreading fats (including low-fat spreads), cooking oils, oil-based salad dressings, mayonnaise, cream, chocolate, crisps, biscuits, pastries, cakes, puddings, ice cream, rich sauces and gravies.

Provide fat, essential fatty acids, some vitamins.

Eat foods containing fat sparingly and look out for the low-fat alternatives.
Sugar:
Soft drinks, sweets, jam, honey, marmalade, biscuits, pastries, cakes, puddings, ice cream.

Provide carbohydrate, some minerals and vitamins and fat in some products (but not others).

Foods and drinks containing sugar should not be consumed too often.

The Whole Diet Approach

Enjoying a wide variety of foods will help to ensure that requirements for energy and nutrients are met on a daily basis. A diet containing a limited number of foods or only small servings will not achieve this goal, and it certainly will not support a strenuous cycling programme. Putting foods into groups according to the main nutrients they contain can help cyclists to choose wisely and enjoyably. Of course, how much is eaten will depend on an individual cyclist's energy and nutrient requirements.

Conclusion

Cyclists should look upon their nutrition as 'healthy eating plus'. Build on what everybody should be doing to maintain good health and make fine adjustments to food and fluid intakes in relation to cycling. The following chapters will help enormously!

The eatwell plate

Use the eatwell plate to help you get the balance right. It shows how much of what you eat should come from each food group.

The eatwell plate, Food Standards Agency. © Crown copyright material, reproduced with the permission of the Controller of HMSO and Queen's Printer for Scotland.

Case Study 1: Jonathan

I am a commuter cyclist riding on a canal towpath and busy London roads during the rush hour. The journey is 7.8 miles and takes me around 35 minutes. I also cycle every other weekend with a cycling club. Those trips are around 25 miles and are definitely 'leisurely'. On my daily commutes to work I have the same every morning for breakfast: two strong coffees and a bowl of porridge mixed with raw bran flakes and muesli. I sometimes have a banana with it. I rarely deviate from this. I eat for good dietary reasons and not due to considering the benefits of fuel or energy. I normally have another coffee at work and then several glasses of water or fruit juice during the day. I usually have soup and vegetables and sometimes wholegrain rice for lunch as I am conscious of trying to reduce my calorie intake. I normally have a glass of water just before setting off for home. I don't bring a bottle of fluid with me for the journey. It's not the carefully planned calorie-controlled, balanced and energy-efficient diet of a competitive cyclist but a middle-aged commuter!

On my weekend trips I usually have coffee and toast, just one slice, preferably wholegrain with olive-derived low-fat spread and jam or marmite. I take a cordial drink 500ml bottle with me. We stop for breakfast around half-way. I find that I am more hungry than usual and will have a cooked breakfast in a café. This would normally consist of toast, poached egg, bacon or sausage.

I have previously ridden long-distance trips on my bike, 50 miles or so. I tend to eat more than usual and will always have a banana or two. I once had some glucose tablets with me which made a huge difference. I can remember feeling very fatigued and my pace really slowed. Around two minutes after taking the glucose tablets my pace quickened and I noticed a boost in my energy and lack of fatigue.

CHAPTER 2

THE CYCLING BODY

Cycling is the most studied sport in terms of physiology and nutrition. Early experiments date back to 1939 when the famous scientists Christensen and Hansen investigated the effect diet had on cycling performance, using static bicycles in the laboratory. The key fact they uncovered was the importance of carbohydrate in exercise performance in relation to both the intensity and duration of the exercise. In their experiments they looked particularly at carbohydrate intake during and after cycling. Their work has become hugely important in highlighting for cyclists (and sportsmen and women generally, regardless of their sport) the need to take on board fuel in the form of carbohydrate during and immediately after cycling.

Cycling is a sport that has one of the highest reported energy costs. Certainly when one looks at the data from the Tour de France, which has twenty stages, covers nearly 4,000km and lasts around three weeks, this becomes very apparent. It has been calculated that during the long 300km stages energy expenditure can be as much as 8,300kcal a day. To put this into perspective, the UK Dietary Reference Values (DRVs) put the estimated average energy requirement (EAR) for men at 2,550kcal a day and for women at 1,940kcal a day.

The main energy source for cycling comes from dietary carbohydrate, which can cause potential problems for some cyclists who have particularly high energy requirements. A diet that is high in energy, primarily from carbohydrate,

Dietary carbohydrate, e.g. from a banana, is the main energy source for cyclists.

is not only extremely bulky but also involves a lot of eating, which will take up time – and time may very well be at a premium. Hard exercise is known to depress appetite and this can make it even more difficult to meet the required energy intake. There is anecdotal evidence to suggest that riders who lose weight during the Tour de France may not actually finish the race. Generally, cycling is considered to have one of the highest energy turnovers across all sports, with races lasting in duration anything from an hour to ultra-endurance events of between six and ten hours.

From food to fuel

Digestion is the process that reduces food mechanically and chemically into a form that can be absorbed into the bloodstream and transported to a variety of destinations in the body. Chewing starts the breakdown of food with saliva mixing in to make swallowing easier.

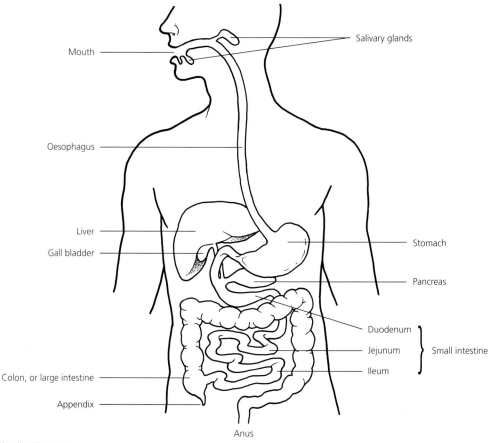

The digestive system.

Saliva also contains an enzyme that begins the digestion of carbohydrate. Food passes from the mouth down the oesophagus or gullet, a musculo-membranous canal about 9 inches long, into the stomach in about three seconds. The main function of the stomach is to break down the food mechanically and through the presence of hydrochloric acid, to kill any bacteria present in the food. Food can remain in the stomach for anything between an hour and four hours as only small amounts are released into the small intestine at a time – in other words, no dumping. Carbohydrate-rich foods pass out of the stomach faster than high-fat foods, with liquids usually passing fastest of all. This is a useful fact for cyclists to remember! Another useful fact is that the rate of stomach emptying can be slowed by stress or nerves. Obviously this may be particularly relevant on race days. Very little else is absorbed from the stomach apart from water and alcohol.

Most of the digestion and absorption processes take place in the small intestine, which is made up of the duodenum, jejunum and ileum. Here fat is broken down into very small droplets by bile, which is produced in the liver but stored in the gall bladder.

The pancreas, a large elongated glandular organ situated behind the stomach, produces juices that neutralize the acidic stomach contents, break down fats into fatty acids, proteins into peptides and amino acids, and starch into maltose. Intestinal juices produced in the wall of the small intestine complete the breakdown of carbohydrate into the simple sugars, glucose, fructose and galactose. The final stage of digestion takes place in the large intestine, which is made up of the colon, rectum and anus. Here water that has been used in the digestion process is reabsorbed and bacteria that are present in the colon break down fibre residues such as cellulose. This is a fermentation process that results in the production of gases and fatty acids. Water continues to be reabsorbed and the residue from digestion, here politely referred to as faeces, becomes more solid and eventually is passed along the rectum to the anus. Food can take anything between one and three days to travel from mouth to anus. Curious cyclists can check their transit time (time from mouth to anus) by eating sweetcorn, as the outer yellow husk is not digested! This information may be useful, particularly on long training cycles or for competition.

Absorption of nutrients – peptides and amino acids from protein, fatty acids from fats, and glucose, fructose and galactose from carbohydrates – takes place primarily through the walls of the small intestine. Only small amounts of water, alcohol, B vitamins, vitamin C and salt can pass through the stomach lining into the bloodstream.

The fate of major nutrients in the body

Carbohydrates

- Transported to all cells; provide energy
- Converted into glycogen; stored in the liver and muscles; readily available source of energy
- Converted into fatty acids; stored as body fat; potential energy source

Fats

- Rebuilt into triglycerides
- Carried by lymphatic system (a system of blind-ending vessels which drain excess tissue fluid from the extracellular space) to blood
- Stored as body fat
- Triglycerides stored in muscle

Proteins

- Amino acids carried to the liver
- Join the amino acid pool in the circulation
- Converted into other amino acids
- Oxidized for energy, often after conversion into glucose, or converted and stored as fat.

The energy systems

Phosphagen energy system
ADP + CP (creatine phosphate) →
C (creatine) + ATP → Energy

Anaerobic glycolytic system
ADP + glucose → ATP + lactic acid →
Energy

Aerobic energy system
Glucose/fatty acids + oxygen → ATP →
Energy + carbon dioxide + water

Energy production

Muscle activity is fuelled by adenosine triphosphate (ATP), a chemical that the body can produce by three different energy systems.

The phosphagen energy system provides energy for explosive manoeuvres or short bursts of cycling, such as riding up a hill. Muscles are only able to store small quantities of creatine phosphate, just enough energy for high-intensity cycling lasting about ten seconds.

The anaerobic glycolytic system breaks down muscle glycogen (the scientific name for stored carbohydrate) into ATP and lactic acid. This system supplies energy for high-intensity cycling lasting two to three minutes. Accumulation of lactic acid leads to muscle fatigue and a drastic and often very noticeable drop in cycling performance. A cyclist will only be able to recover by dropping the intensity and basically cycling more slowly for a period of time. This is the equivalent of going from running down to jogging or even slowing up to a walking pace. This reduction in exercise intensity allows the lactic acid to be converted into less toxic substances, which can then be removed via the bloodstream.

The aerobic system uses oxygen with carbohydrate and fat to produce ATP. This system can continue to produce energy from two or three minutes up to several hours. In other words, it is the energy system used particularly for all medium- or low-intensity cycling. Carbon dioxide and water, the by-products of this system, are absorbed in the bloodstream and removed. Elite level cyclists have a high aerobic capacity. But provision of energy is not just about fuelling the muscles: the importance of the mental aspects of cycling are just as vital. These need energy too, though not as much!

It is more efficient for the body to use carbohydrate rather than fat because it produces more energy for a given amount of oxygen. However, the downside is that the muscles can only store a limited amount of carbohydrate. This is very different from fat storage, where there appears to be no limit to the amount that can be stored in the body. As stores of glycogen become more and more depleted, the rate of ATP production slows and power output drops. At a slower cycling speed oxidation of fatty acids can be used to meet more of the energy demand. Cyclists call it 'bonking', runners call it 'hitting the wall'.

• • • • • • •

Fatigue

There can be several possible causes of fatigue or tiredness, some related to cycling and others not related at all. An obvious cause is not getting enough hours of sleep on a regular basis. The ideal is probably at least eight hours every night. A poor sleep pattern may be due to a number of factors, including stress, emotional problems and medical conditions such as depression. Relating to cycling, fatigue can be caused by over-training or an over-zealous weight loss programme resulting in too much weight being lost too quickly. Intentional rapid weight loss of more than 2lb a week can certainly lead to tiredness or fatigue. A cyclist who does not eat enough carbohydrate to replace losses in muscle glycogen stores through cycling or other training sessions such as gym workouts or runs will also experience their performance taking a dive – probably a very significant one. If other cyclists or family members comment on this drop in performance or remark how tired the cyclist looks, he or she would do well to take heed!

Symptoms of fatigue caused by poor carbohydrate intake include muscle heaviness, poor energy levels in training, a feeling of enormous effort without the expected result and increasing tiredness as the week goes on.

Fatigue that continues for a month or even longer could be caused by an underlying medical problem, not necessarily related to cycling. A check-up at the doctor's surgery, explaining the symptoms and any lifestyle issues, should highlight any medical reasons for the tiredness. These can include anaemia, infection, depression or an under-active thyroid gland. A GP will be able to help once a diagnosis or reason for the overwhelming tiredness has been identified.

• • • • •
Sleep

Sleep plays an important part in the recovery process after training sessions or races. Research shows that people who engage in an active lifestyle sleep longer and deeper than less active people. Only essential functions continue during sleep. However, any physiological repair and growth, if applicable, will also take place. This growth and repair process tends to peak during the periods of deep sleep.

There can be a number of reasons why a cyclist might have trouble getting to sleep. Hard training in the evening after a day working or studying can affect sleep patterns. Worrying the night before a race or just general worries often lead to a restless night and of course being away

Practical ways to ensure a good night's sleep

- Have a pre-sleep routine.
- Go to bed at the same time every night when possible and get up at the same time every morning, including at weekends.
- Include a 'catch-up' night if necessary, by going to bed earlier and getting up later. Remember to tell family or flat-mates of the change in routine though!
- Keep any daytime naps to less than an hour.
- Try to be quiet and still for fifteen minutes before trying to sleep, either reading or listening to soft, gentle music. Avoid doing brain-stimulating puzzles or crosswords – save these for daylight hours!
- Have a high-carbohydrate snack before bed (toast, cereal, banana). Avoid high-fat foods and fast foods late at night (e.g. doner kebabs).
- Have a glass of milk or a mug of hot chocolate made with milk: a small amount of protein can encourage sleep.
- Try drinking camomile tea at bedtime – it is a very soothing drink.
- Take a warm bath or shower.
- Create the optimum environment for sleep: keep the bedroom quiet, dark and cool (18°C/65°F).
- Sleep in a bigger bed rather than a narrow one. (As there can be between forty and sixty position changes in the night, this would seem sensible.)
- Lavender drops on the pillow can help some people.
- Use relaxation techniques or reading to get to sleep – but no scary books! Avoid noisy or violent films late at night, loud music through headphones and even counting sheep (i.e. avoid any brain stimulation).

from home and sleeping in a strange bed with different noises (or no noises at all) can all affect the quality and quantity of sleep. How much sleep is needed is a very individual thing. There is no magic number of hours needed though most adults find eight or more hours better than fewer than eight – certainly on a regular basis. Both the quantity and quality of sleep tend to reduce with age and daytime naps become quite appealing! A small amount of alcohol before bed can help some people but an excess can definitely hinder. Similarly a high intake of caffeine could interfere with sleep patterns, particularly in those not used to drinking a caffeinated drink at bedtime.

Immune function

It is important that a cyclist maintains a healthy immune system as this will help protect the body from bacterial or viral infections. It will also help in the recovery from any injuries picked up while cycling. The immune system is made up of a network of physical barriers (the skin and tissues in the lung, nose and intestines), chemical barriers (the acidity of the stomach) and specific cells called phagocytes. These cells have the ability to engulf and digest unwanted and harmful particles or cells that the body neither needs nor wants.

Moderate physical activity has a positive effect on the immune system. For example, surveys have shown that people who walk at a good pace for thirty to forty-five minutes five times a week have fewer days off work because of a heavy cold or chest infection than their fellow workmates who live very inactive lifestyles. However, cyclists who have very heavy training schedules could be at risk of picking up an upper respiratory tract infection (URTI), especially after a hard session lasting up to ninety minutes. This is because such training schedules can suppress the immune system, thus making the body much more susceptible to infections. This probably applies particularly to cyclists with young families or teachers – in other words those spending a lot of contact time with small, snuffling children! The risk of picking up an infection can be exacerbated if a cyclist is not getting a regular good night's sleep, is feeling stressed, is not eating well or is attempting to lose weight too quickly.

Case Study 2: Annie

How I prepare nutritionally before and/or after training

When preparing for training I usually take a piece of food for each hour I intend to train for, usually opting for things like cereal bars and cake; I tend to leave the gels for racing only. I have learnt over the years that there is no point putting something in your back pocket that you don't like the taste of, as you will be less inclined to eat it, which will inevitably lead to 'hitting the wall'.

After training it depends very much on the time available; if I am rushed and know I have a hard training session the next day, I will opt for the convenience of a recovery shake. If I have more time available I will always opt for a proper meal as I find it more satisfying. I usually go for some kind of sandwich, often chicken, or quick and easy beans on toast. I find that if I have fuelled correctly during training I do not need a huge meal.

How to cope with maintaining hydration while cycling

Hydrating whilst training can be difficult, especially during racing or training sessions where you find yourself constantly on the limit. Grabbing sips at every opportunity is important, so at traffic lights or between blocks of intervals I tend to take a sip. I usually find if I drink too much too fast I tend to feel it sloshing around in my stomach, which isn't pleasant. I aim to drink a small bottle per hour, but this depends on the temperature. Sometimes during long training rides lasting four hours or more it's just not possible to carry enough fluid to maintain hydration, and so a real emphasis needs to be put on rehydrating when I get home. I tend to take one bottle made up with energy powder and one bottle of just water. Too much energy drink can sometimes upset my stomach and too much water is boring and doesn't replace salts lost in sweat, so I have a compromise.

A few anecdotes

When racing abroad, cyclists are often faced with the hotel buffet: an array of food both beneficial and detrimental to your race performance, as one of my teammates found out. At the European championships in Turkey the buffet stretched for what seemed miles, and using your head and not your heart to select your food was a challenge. My teammate unfortunately went with his heart and piled onto his plate a beef stroganoff dish, mainly because it had tiny French fries in it. Needless to say this wasn't the best choice and in fact during the race his stomach actually swelled to the size of that of a pregnant lady and resulted in a DNF. Moral of the story: pick familiar, sensible foods for your pre-race meals and don't be lured in by the buffet.

It is always important when preparing bottles for racing to mark them up clearly before giving them to your pit team or *soigneur* to hand to you during a race. Imagine the surprise of being handed up a thick, lumpy recovery drink during a baking hot road race in France with no clue if or when you will get your hands on another. It was a tough decision whether to succumb to dehydration or try to stomach the hot, chocolatey paste. Thankfully, teammates came to the rescue and we managed to ration the available drink between us; needless to say the recovery drink was thrown to some poor unsuspecting French kid.

When training sessions are hard, your focus tends to be on the effort and most often the pain, rather than keeping on top of nutrition and hydration. This was particularly the case when I was training with a gold medallist in the women's team pursuit from London 2012. That day, I understood why she was Olympic champion as I clung to her wheel for the duration of the three-hour ride, not daring to ease up to take a breath and take on board some food for embarrassment of being dropped. Due to this cyclist ego I found myself in an even worse situation, when around fifteen minutes from home I completely and dramatically 'hit the wall' – not for love nor money could I turn the pedals or see straight for that matter. I proceeded to have to be pushed single-handedly all the way home, through busy town centres just to rub it in that bit more. In hindsight, I wish I had remembered to just reach into my back pocket and pull out some food and I could have stood more chance of avoiding embarrassment.

CHAPTER 3

TRAINING DIET

Professional and serious amateur cyclists train at least twenty hours a week, while most amateurs train about ten hours a week. Energy and nutrient requirements vary according to the volume and intensity of training but also the type of cycling, i.e. track, road, BMX or mountain biking. The key nutritional goal is to achieve high energy and carbohydrate intakes to meet the training loads, taking into account the practicalities of fitting refuelling and meals into a hectic lifestyle. There must be an adequate fuel intake during training and refuelling after training, but the overall diet must still be a well-balanced one that meets all the requirements for protein, vitamins, minerals and essential fatty acids, even dietary fibre.

Sprint cycling is a very high-intensity, short duration form of exercise. Energy intake will be based on the demands of training with a carbohydrate intake of 6–8g/kg body-weight/per day, which will be approximately 65 per cent of the total daily calorie intake.

Distance cyclists need a greater carbohydrate intake of 8–10g/kg body-weight/per day, of which a significant amount must be consumed during cycling. Cyclists therefore need to acquire the skill of 'eating on the bike'. For them carbohydrate/electrolyte drinks, energy bars (solid rather than crumbly), gels, rice cakes and bananas are suitable choices but sticky foods should be avoided, as should foods with a high fat content. However, cyclists need to find what works best for them – meeting the nutritional requirements but also remaining palatable during the various stages of the ride. What a cyclist might enjoy early on, from about thirty minutes into the ride, may not taste so good during the later stages of the ride. Cyclists should not wait until they start to feel tired before they take on board carbohydrate. It will help a little but it would be far more effective to start to consume carbohydrate earlier, before tiredness kicks in, and to continue to do so throughout the ride.

After training sessions muscle glycogen stores must be topped up. A cyclist whose appetite is depressed after a hard cycle ride could use a liquid meal replacement drink.

Knowing the weight or household measure of good sources of carbohydrate that provide 50g of carbohydrate can help a cyclist to work out approximately how much they need to eat to meet their daily requirement for carbohydrate – a ball park figure will be more than adequate!

Good sources of carbohydrate for meals, snacks and refuellers

Cereals – any variety, including hot cereals like porridge

Bread – including bagels, English muffins, crumpets, pikelets, naans, chapattis, potato cakes, raisin bread, malt loaf, rye bread, tea breads, pancakes, Scotch pancakes, tortillas and wraps, soft pretzels and rice cakes

Fruit muffins, fruit bread

Crispbreads, water biscuits, oatcakes, crackers, rice cakes and matzos

Pasta and noodles

Rice

Potatoes

Sweet potatoes, yam, cassava, plantains

Polenta, couscous, oatmeal, bulgur wheat, millet and quinoa

Pizza bases (ideally thick base)

Beans – baked, butter, red kidney, borlotti, cannelloni and mixed

Peas, lentils, pearl barley, chickpeas

Sweetcorn

Carrots, parsnips, swedes, turnips, beetroot

Fruit – fresh, dried, canned or cooked

Jam, marmalade, honey, fruit spreads, golden syrup, maple syrup, molasses, black treacle

Twiglets, sesame sticks, Japanese rice crackers, breadsticks, pretzels

Biscuits – Jaffa cakes, fig rolls, garibaldi, rich tea, plain digestives

Cakes – currant buns, tea cakes, iced buns, Chelsea buns, plain or fruit scones, fruit cake and fruit loaf, gingerbread, parkin, jam-filled Swiss roll, flapjacks and other similar 'simple or plain' cakes

Breakfast, cereal, muesli and cake bars

Popcorn

Puddings – fruit crumbles, bread pudding, milk puddings, jelly and custard, banana and custard, meringues, ice-cream

Yoghurt – fruit and natural

Milk, flavoured milk, milk shakes and smoothies

Sweetened soft drinks – squash, cordial, canned drinks

Fruit juice

Having this information is one thing, implementing it is quite another. The following are practical ways a cyclist can boost their carbohydrate intake:

Eat frequently! Have regular meals, mini-meals and refuellers throughout the day.

Base every eating occasion around a carbohydrate-rich food. Make it the biggest portion of the meal.

Use thick sliced bread rather than medium or thin sliced.

Have bread as well as pasta, rice or potatoes with meals on hard training days.

Jam, marmalade, honey and fruit spreads provide carbohydrate but no fat. They should be spread thickly and the fat thinly.

Boiled, mashed or jacket potatoes are low in fat, chips are not. Thick cut oven varieties are the best chip choice.

Portions of food providing approx. 50g carbohydrate*

Food	Weight (approx)	Household measure
Porridge oats	75g (uncooked weight)	5 tablespoons
Wholewheat biscuits	65g	3–4 biscuits
Muesli	70g	5 tablespoons
Cornflake type cereals	60g	10 tablespoons
Semi-skimmed milk	1⅔ pints/950ml	
Unsweetened orange juice	1 pint/568ml	
Breads and bakery goods		
Bread, large, medium sliced	100g	3 slices
Bread, large, thick sliced	100g	2½ slices
Bagel	70g	1
Rolls	100g	2
Baps (very large rolls)	100g	1
Pitta bread, large	95g	1
Pretzel (soft)	100g	1
Potato cake	135g	2½ cakes
Crumpets	125g	3
Fruit scone	100g	2
Currant buns	100g	2
Malt loaf	100g	2½ slices
Pasta (cooked)	225g (70g uncooked)	8 tablespoons
Rice (cooked)	175g (60g uncooked)	4 heaped tablespoons
Pizza base (thick)	½ large (9in)	
Potatoes		
Boiled	300g	5 egg sized
Jacket	175g	1 medium (with skin)
Mashed	325g	7 heaped tablespoons
Oven chips	175g	approx 20
Fruit		
Apples	4 medium	
Bananas	2 large	
Dried apricots	100g	15
Dried dates	100g	7
Figs	100g	5
Raisins	70g	2½ tablespoons
Sultanas	70g	2½ tablespoons

* Information about manufactured products can be found on the food labels.

Sweet potatoes, plantains and cassava can make an interesting change to potatoes.

Rice is not difficult to cook but brown rice is easier and parboiled easiest, though more expensive.

Cook rice in bulk and freeze portions. Frozen rice can be reheated in a minute in a microwave.

Use different shapes of pasta to relieve boredom. Melted low-fat soft cheese makes a very quick pasta sauce to which cooked chicken, ham or canned tuna can be added.

Extra pasta or rice can be turned into a lunch the following day.

Get out of the pasta rut and experiment with bulgur wheat, couscous and polenta – all available in pre-cooked forms.

Breakfast cereals can be eaten at any time, even just before bed.

Breakfast cereal and fruit juice complement each other. Both provide carbohydrate and the vitamin C in the juice helps iron absorption from the cereal.

Red kidney beans, borlotti beans, cannelloni beans, chickpeas and sweetcorn can be added to canned vegetable or minestrone soups; to tomato sauces with pasta; to curry sauces with rice. They all add protein to the meal, too.

Baked beans on toast makes a quick and easy meal, again providing carbohydrate and protein. Warm pitta bread can be used for a change.

Frozen pitta bread can be warmed from frozen quickly in a toaster or under the grill.

Add fresh (especially bananas), canned or dried fruit to breakfast cereal, have canned fruit and low-fat custard or try a banana sandwich.

Low-fat milkshakes (e.g. semi-skimmed milk, low-fat yoghurt and a banana) or just an extra pint of semi-skimmed milk will provide quality protein too.

Protein intake

Protein intake requirements are the same for both speed and endurance cyclists, set at between 1.2g and 1.6g/kg body-weight/per day. Dietary surveys suggest that most athletes (including cyclists) meet these requirements without difficulty and without the use of protein supplements. Consuming protein soon after exercise begins the process of muscle protein synthesis. Sources of animal protein appear to be particularly helpful and an intake of just 20–25g protein appears to be enough to maximize this response to exercise. Studies using milk not only as a fluid to rehydrate but in relation to post-exercise protein synthesis have produced very favourable results (*see* Chapter 3 References, 1 and 2). Milk provides good-quality protein and amongst the essential amino acids making up the protein, leucine particularly has attracted interest amongst researchers. For example, taking leucine on board after resistance training has been shown to enhance protein synthesis. Consuming protein post-exercise does not negate the need to refuel with carbohydrate. The alternative to the many supplements that some sportspeople take to ensure glycogen resynthesis and protein synthesis could be something as simple as a bowl of breakfast cereal with milk, followed a few hours later by a meal.

Calculating daily protein requirements

The following information shows the quantity of everyday protein-rich foods that provide 20g of protein. Having worked out the target daily protein intake (body-weight in kg × requirement in g), it should be possible, using the information below, to build up daily protein intake using a variety of different foods.

Protein-rich foods such as nuts and seeds will not be eaten in large enough amounts to contribute 20g protein. However, they are still useful sources of protein and it is worth noting how much needs to be eaten to provide 10g protein.

Other foods included in the diet for their carbohydrate content will also contribute protein, so it would sensible to err on the side of less rather than more!

Daily protein requirements

Food	Weight of food	Portion of food
Beef, lamb, pork	75g	2 medium slices
Chicken or turkey	75g	1 small breast
Fish (cod, haddock, etc.)	100g	1 medium fillet
Salmon	100g	1 average steak
Mackerel	100g	1 small fillet
Fishfingers	135g	5 fingers
Tuna in brine	100g	1 small can
Prawns, boiled, no shell	100g	approx 30 small prawns
Semi/skimmed milk	600ml	1 pint
Skimmed milk powder	40g	4 tablespoons
Soy	700ml	A generous pint
Cheddar cheese, reduced fat	60g	2 matchbox-sized pieces
Low-fat fruit yoghurt	400g	2 x 200g pots
Eggs	3 x size 2 eggs	
Baked beans	400g	1 large can
Lentils, cooked or canned	265g	6½ tablespoons
Chickpeas, cooked or canned	270g	7½ tablespoons
Red kidney beans, cooked or canned	290g	8 tablespoons

Food	Weight of food	Portion of food
Brazil nuts	70g	21 nuts
Cashew nuts	50g	50 whole nuts
Plain peanuts	40g	30 whole nuts
Peanut butter	40g	thickly spread on 2 slices bread
Seeds	50g	
Trail mix (average)	50g	
Walnuts	70g	21 halves

Eggs are another food to highlight as a good source of protein. They have a high biological value, which means they contain all the essential amino acids (building blocks of protein) that our bodies need, as well as a wide range of other nutrients (vitamins A, D, E and many B vitamins, as well as the minerals iron, phosphorus and zinc). Many people consider that eggs are high-fat foods but nothing could be further from the truth! A medium egg (59g) provides 80kcal and has a fat content of 5.8g, of which only 1.7g is saturated fat. Discarding the yolk means the majority of the nutrients are also thrown away. Eggs are useful for cyclists with little time to prepare meals; they are quick and easy to cook, and can be prepared in a variety of different ways.

. . . .

Fat in the diet

Energy requirements for cyclists can be quite high but this should not be taken as an excuse to indulge in high intakes of food. Fat stored as adipose tissue can only be used as a source of fuel for the lowest-intensity exercise or very prolonged endurance exercise. There may be a few exceptions but for the vast majority of cyclists the priority fuel remains carbohydrate.

The following are some practical hints to help keep fat intake under reasonable control:

- Choose a low-fat spread rather than butter, hard margarine or soft margarine but still spread it thinly (particularly as several slices of bread may be eaten per day)
- It may not be necessary to use any type of butter or spread on bread or toast, for example with baked beans on toast, or peanut butter or honey sandwiches
- Semi-skimmed milk not only has less fat but more protein and calcium than whole milk
- Use either reduced fat cheeses or less of a strongly flavoured cheese
- Grate cheese for sandwiches or toasted cheese – it goes further

- Use low-fat or reduced fat salad cream or mayonnaise when possible
- Make 'creamy' sauces by gently melting low-fat soft cheese
- Cut down on crisps, chocolate, pastries and 'rich' cakes and biscuits. Snack on carbohydrate foods, such as fruit (fresh or dried), sandwiches with low-fat fillings, 'plain' cakes and biscuits (currant buns, scones, tea bread, crumpets, rich tea biscuits, fig rolls, plain digestives, Jaffa cakes, etc.)
- Eat fish more often – but grilled, microwaved, steamed or baked rather than deep-fried in batter; grill fish cakes and fishfingers
- Chicken and turkey are low in fat, especially if the skin is not eaten. Most of the fat is found underneath and is discarded when the skin is removed (before or after cooking)
- Buy the leanest affordable cuts of meat and trim off any visible fat (before or after cooking)
- Use any cooking method other than frying
- Meat products such as sausages and beefburgers can be fatty, so do not eat them too often
- Meat pies, sausage rolls and pasties contain a lot of fat in the meat and in the pastry, so limit intake of these foods as much as possible
- Keep pastry to one layer – top or bottom crust only
- Measure out oil when cooking – don't just pour from the container
- Stir-frying needs hardly any oil
- Use non-stick pans to cut down the need for oil (and make washing-up easier too)
- Flavour foods with low oil dressings, lemon or lime juice, balsamic vinegar, tomato ketchup or mustard
- Best chip choice is thick, oven chips (5 per cent sunflower oil)
- Keep junk/fast food to a minimum.

Iron in the diet

Haem iron is found in meat and meat products and non-haem iron in cereals, vegetables, peas, beans and lentils and fruits. Haem iron is well absorbed, up to 20–40 per cent being taken up, but only 5–20 per cent of iron from vegetable sources, eggs and milk is absorbed. Many people avoid meat because of the perceived fat content, but in fact the fat content of lean red meat has fallen by a third over the last twenty years. An individual may not eat meat for a variety of good reasons but fat content is not a valid one.

Practical ways to increase iron intake

Eating red meat, if appropriate, is the easiest way to ensure an adequate iron intake. Breakfast cereals fortified with iron are a good choice, especially as they are usually eaten very regularly in good amounts. Vitamin C helps the absorption

Good sources of iron in the diet

Animal sources:

2 slices liver (100g) 9mg

1 whole pig's kidney (140g) 9mg

1 portion black pudding (75g) 15mg

8oz/225g lean beef steak 6mg

4oz/100g lean minced beef 2.7mg

2 thick slices corned beef 2.9mg

Pâté, low-fat on bread (40g) 2.5mg

1 chicken breast 0.65mg

1 chicken quarter 2.0mg

1 small can tuna in brine 1.0mg

1 large fillet white fish 0.5mg

size 3 egg 1.1mg

Cereals:

2 slices white bread 1.0mg

2 slices wholemeal bread 1.9mg

Breakfast cereals*

Pasta, cooked average portion (7½ tablespoons) 1.8mg

Rice, cooked average portion (4½ tablespoons) 0.4mg

Vegetables and pulses:

Average portion spinach 1.7mg

Large portion cabbage 0.7mg

Large portion peas 1.4mg

225g can baked beans in tomato sauce 3.2mg

120g cooked red lentils (3 tablespoons) 2.9mg

120g cooked brown/green lentils (3 tablespoons) 4.2mg

Average portion tofu (bean curd) 0.7mg

Nuts:

25g bag cashew nuts 1.6mg

1 tablespoon sesame seeds 1.1mg

Fruit:

12 ready to eat dried apricots 3.4mg

6 dried dates 1.0mg

2 tablespoons raisins 0.8mg

* Many breakfast cereals are enriched with iron. Check the nutritional information panel on the box.

of iron; including orange or grapefruit juice with breakfast cereals, adding tomatoes and peppers to sandwiches and cooked dishes, and drinking squashes containing added vitamin C with meals can all help boost intake. Strong tea and coffee should be drunk between meals, not with them, as the tannins present can reduce iron absorption. Absorption of iron from vegetables and cereals can be improved by eating a source of animal protein such as red meat at the same meal. Wholegrain breads and cereals are better choices than those with added bran as excessive bran intake can also reduce iron absorption.

Non-meat eaters should ensure that their diet contains some of the following on a daily basis: wholegrain cereals and flours (wheat, rye, millet, oatmeal), nuts (almonds, brazils, cashews, hazelnuts), dark green leafy vegetables (cabbage, watercress, spinach, broccoli).

Oily fish

Oily fish may not be the most popular food but it should be included in the weekly diet if possible as it contains omega-3 fatty acids which not only have an impact on heart health but have the potential to relieve symptoms of stiffness and pain in joints. Ideally two portions (280g) of oily fish such as salmon, canned sardines, herring, mackerel, fresh tuna (but not canned tuna) or trout should be eaten every week.

Recovery

What a cyclist eats and drinks after cycling can help him or her to recover from the training session so that maximum effort can be put into the next training session, whether it is later that day or the next day. It also helps the body adapt to the training load. Potential problems in achieving full recovery include lack of appetite, particularly after a hard high-intensity session, as well as a lack in availability of suitable foods and fluids.

> **Key issues post-training and aims of recovery**
>
> *Issues:*
> Depletion of muscle glycogen stores
> Dehydration
> Net loss of protein
> Suppressed immune system
>
> *Recovery:*
> Refuel muscle (and liver) glycogen
> Restore fluids and electrolytes
> Repair muscle tissue
> Encourage adaptation process
> Boost immune system

Replacement of muscle glycogen stores is fastest in the first hour after exercise and the general advice is always to start the refuelling process during this time. Recommendations are to aim for an intake of 1–1.2g carbohydrate per kg body-weight. Recent evidence suggests that small intakes every fifteen to twenty minutes of moderate to high glycaemic index foods may help the replacement even more. Including protein with the carbohydrate helps muscle recovery and reduces protein breakdown. With a net loss of muscle protein there is also a need to rebuild muscle in the first one to two hours after exercise, not unlike the muscle glycogen scenario. Aim for 15–25g good-quality protein during the first hour after training. Carbohydrate post-exercise is obviously vital from the point of view of refuelling, but studies have shown that it can also play a part in reducing the amount of muscle protein breakdown. It also reduces the stress hormone response to exercise, which therefore helps protect the immune system, as well as providing fuel (glucose) for the immune system, specifically the white blood cells.

Dairy products are becoming more and more popular as aids to post-exercise recovery: low-fat milk provides both carbohydrate and protein. Practically it is widely available, cheap and, to provide variety, can be flavoured with milkshake syrups if wished. Total daily carbohydrate intake still remains the key. Depending on the amount and intensity of training, this can be 7–12g carbohydrate per kg body-weight per day to ensure that glycogen stores are adequate. A pint of milk and two medium bananas after a hard training session will provide approximately 20g protein and 50g carbohydrate. Alternatively, a commercial recovery sports drink containing whey and casein

could be used. Keeping to the same flavour can lead to 'flavour fatigue'. It is therefore a good idea to remain open to other options.

> **Suitable snack food to store in panniers or back-packs**
> Cereal, breakfast, energy or sports bars
> Jaffa cakes
> Twiglets or pretzels (salted)
> Fig rolls, Swiss rolls, malt loaf (or similar items according to taste)
> Fresh fruit – particularly bananas (stored so they do not get squashed)
> Dried fruit

Meal planning

A busy lifestyle can sometimes lead to a chaotic, poorly planned diet. Taking a little time to plan a weekly menu can help enormously, as shopping can be done for the week in one go, though perhaps with some top-ups for more fresh food during the week. Cooking foods such as mince in bulk and then freezing it in meal-sized portions can save a lot of time. Defrosting in a microwave will be no problem but if the mince needs to thaw out naturally, it must be taken out of the freezer several hours before cooking to defrost completely. Ready meals can be a useful option if there is not time to prepare, cook and eat. Supermarkets sell a good range of suitable, healthy meals (with 'healthy' often highlighted on the packaging), which are usually microwaveable. Portions can be small, so two may be needed to make up a reasonable serving, perhaps with some bread on the side. Use the information in the Appendix to help plan, shop, store and cook!

A typical day's diet plan for a road racer

Breakfast – Porridge made with skimmed milk, topped with blueberries and a spoon of milled mixed seeds

On the bike (4 hours) – 2 bananas, 2 flapjack bars, 2 bottles of sports drinks and 2 bottles of water

Recovery drink/lunch – Recovery drink: milkshake made from 500ml of milk, 100g frozen fruit and a banana; lunch: medium jacket potato, tinned tuna and mixed salad

Mid-afternoon snack – Either yoghurt, or something like a hot milky drink and a small piece of cake

Evening meal – Chicken or red meat, rice, mixed vegetables and salad

Supper – Small bowl of cereal with skimmed milk

Written by Nigel Mitchell, Head of Nutrition at British Cycling/Team Sky, and reproduced by kind permission of the Dairy Council.

Alcohol

Alcohol affects the body in a number of ways, many of which have a direct impact on sport and exercise performance. It stimulates the heart to beat faster; widens the blood vessels (causing flushing and a warm sensation); diverts blood to the skin causing loss of body heat; stimulates gastric juices; and depresses the nervous system, which has many negative effects on performance. Also, of course, long-term drinking can seriously damage the heart and liver.

The effects of alcohol are dose related. If only one or two drinks have been enjoyed the night before exercising, reaction time, strength, power and cardiovascular performance will not be particularly affected the next day. But drinking more than this will have an effect! It impairs balance, co-ordination, reaction times and visual perception, as well as having a negative effect on strength, power, muscle endurance and aerobic endurance. Body temperature regulation may also be impaired during a long cycle ride in the cold.

How alcohol affects fuel supplies

Alcohol is not used to a great extent as a source of fuel during exercise. It is metabolized in the liver and though the breakdown products may end up in muscle, they do not seem important as an energy source. This is probably because it requires a lot more oxygen to release energy from alcohol than from an equivalent amount of carbohydrate or fat. The liver metabolizes alcohol at a slow, set rate, which makes it of little use when a rapid energy source is needed to fuel exercise, particularly moderate to high-intensity exercise. During prolonged exercise alcohol interferes with glucose metabolism. When the liver metabolizes alcohol, glucose output falls and the risk of developing hypoglycaemia (low blood glucose level) increases. Fuel starts to run out sooner, fatigue sets in and exercise intensity falls. Lastly, it is not possible to speed up the breakdown of alcohol by exercising harder, nor can alcohol be 'sweated out'.

Practical advice

Alcohol post-exercise can detract from implementing the key nutritional aspects of recovery – replacing glycogen and rehydrating. Eating and drinking non-alcoholic drinks before starting to drink alcohol is a sensible route to take. Food slows down the rate at which alcohol is absorbed into the bloodstream. Eating at the same time as drinking alcohol can also help to slow the speed of drinking, with the possible result that less might be drunk!

Ways to control alcohol intake

- Pace drinks – alternate an alcohol drink with a non-alcoholic drink.
- Filling up with water or soda first to curb thirst means the first few drinks are likely to go down more slowly.
- Sip rather than gulp.
- Put the glass down between sips if possible.
- Volunteer to be driver.
- Finish each drink and avoid 'topping up' – this brings an element of control into drinking.
- Buying a round? Have a non-alcoholic drink.
- Drink lots of water before bed.

CHAPTER 4

TRAINING FLUIDS

First, some definitions and facts! It is important to start every training session in a euhydrated state – in other words, in water balance. Hyper-hydration is the state of being in positive water balance (water excess) and hypo-hydration is the state of being in negative water balance (water deficit). Losing water from the body is the process of dehydration, whereas rehydration is the process of gaining body water. Euhydration is not a steady state as the body is continually losing water and yet we replace it much more randomly, with time delays. The main ways in which water is lost from the body are in urine, sweat, gastro-intestinal waste contents (faeces) and through breathing.

Rehydration – the process of gaining body water.

Daily water balance in a sedentary individual with a body mass of about 70–75kg living in a temperate climate (References, see Chapter 4, 1)

Daily water input		Daily water losses	
Food	1,000ml	Urine	1250ml
Drinks	1,200ml	Faeces	100ml
Metabolism	350ml	Skin	850ml
Total	2,550ml	Lungs	350ml
		Total	2,550ml

The body gains water from drinks and also from food. The amount of water in different foods varies considerably. The majority of fluid intake comes from drinks, with less but still useful amounts coming from food. Fruit and vegetables have a high water content and eaten regularly they can make a useful contribution to fluid intake. Of course, they do also have other health benefits attributable to the presence of various vitamins and minerals, which indirectly will be beneficial to cycling by helping to keep a cyclist in good health.

Water content of selected foods (g per 100g edible portion)	
Bananas	76g
Butter/margarine	16g
Cheese	36g
Chicken	75g
Chips	57g
Crisps	2g
Eggs	75g
Lettuce	95g
Low-fat spread	50g
Melon	92g
Milk	88g
Oranges	86g
Peanuts	6g
Potatoes	79g
White fish	82g
Yoghurt	77g
(1g equivalent to 1ml)	

The role of water in the body

Water has a key role to play in helping to keep the body alive. The human body can survive for many weeks without food (though it probably does not feel too good doing it) but it cannot survive for more than a few days without water. Water accounts for between 50 and 60 per cent of the total body-weight and it has many and varied functions in the body. It is an essential part of all body cells and a major constituent of all the bodily fluids including blood, sweat and lymph. The *Oxford Dictionary of Sports Science and Medicine* defines the lymphatic system as: 'A system of blind-ending vessels which drain excess tissue fluid from the extracellular space. The lymphatic system

Bodily functions of water
- Transport of nutrients and oxygen
- Elimination of waste by the kidneys in urine
- Temperature regulation by the sweat mechanism
- Swallowing (saliva)
- Digestion (digestive juices)
- Movement of joints and eyes, working as a lubricant
- Transport of sound
- Maintenance of blood volume and blood pressure
- Respiration

contains lymph nodes which remove foreign bodies and produce antibodies, and other lymphoid organs and tissues.' Muscle contains approximately 75 per cent water by weight. Adipose tissue or body fat contains only 5 per cent. Women have larger stores of body fat and therefore less body water than men.

Sweating and sweat losses

Sweat rates can vary a great deal between cyclists, even when they are cycling at the same pace, for the same duration and in the same environmental conditions. It is not just the sweat rate that varies either – the composition of sweat can be quite different too. The concentration of electrolytes (sodium, potassium and chloride) in sweat is lower than in blood, which means that more water than electrolytes is lost from the blood through sweating. Dehydration caused by sweating results in an increase in the concentration of sodium, potassium and chloride in the blood. However, this will only happen if water is not drunk to compensate for the fluid lost in sweat. The combination of large sweat losses and an intake of water alone can lead to an abnormally low concentration of sodium in the blood plasma. (Plasma is the fluid, non-cellular part of blood.)

There are several factors that can affect the rate of sweating and cyclists should take these into account when considering what fluids to take with them on cycle rides, and in what quantities.

Exercise intensity

As exercise intensity increases, the sweat rate also increases. At exercise intensities greater than 75 per cent VO_2, there is a reduction in the rate at which fluid can be digested, absorbed and finally reach the bloodstream. In other words, when the muscles are working hard, the body cuts back on other bodily functions, such as digestion.

Environmental temperature

At higher ambient temperatures sweat losses are greater because the methods normally used to remove heat from the body (conduction, convection and radiation) are unable to cope. A cyclist may be sweating even before starting the ride. In cool conditions sweating may not start until some minutes into the ride. Current literature suggests that endurance exercise in warm conditions (an ambient temperature of >30°C) leads to fluid losses of 2 to 7 per cent body-weight through sweating. This results in a drop in performance, albeit to varying degrees.

In temperate conditions, dehydration of 1 to 2 per cent body-weight is unlikely to have any effect on endurance performance lasting no more than ninety minutes. However, if the level of dehydration becomes greater than 2 per cent of body-weight and the exercise duration is greater than ninety minutes, exercise performance will be impaired.

This level of dehydration seems to have a negative effect on performance in both temperate and hot conditions, particularly when exercise lasts ninety minutes or longer. Cyclists obviously need to work at minimizing dehydration when they are cycling in a hot environment for sixty minutes or more. In cooler environments (20–21°C) cyclists are probably better at tolerating 2 per cent dehydration without any significant drop in performance. In cold environments a cyclist may be able to tolerate dehydration of more than 2 per cent. However, it is always important to remember that there can be considerable variations between individuals, with some cyclists being much better than others at coping in different environmental conditions. Similarly some cyclists may cope better with higher levels of hypohydration (the state of being in negative water balance or water deficit), while others find their performance drops to a much lower level.

Humidity

On a humid day the atmosphere contains more moisture than usual. This has the effect of making the sweat mechanism less effective in cooling the body down. This is because it is the evaporation of sweat from the skin, rather than the actual production of sweat, that cools the skin and in time the body. On humid days sweat does not evaporate from the skin but just drips, and this has no cooling effect on the body, with the ultimate result that fluid is lost but with little body temperature regulation.

Gender differences

Females tend to have smaller plasma volumes. (Plasma is the fluid, non-cellular part of blood.) They also have a lower percentage of body water than most males. If a male and female cyclist were losing sweat at the same rate, the female cyclist would be losing a greater proportion of body water and plasma volume. However, in the same conditions females tend to sweat less than males.

Hydration status

As a cyclist becomes more and more dehydrated, the plasma volume drops, sweat rate is reduced and body temperature regulation becomes less well controlled. This results in the body becoming less able to meet the thermal stress of cycling.

Acclimatization

Training in the heat can help cyclists to adapt to the environment. Adaptation results in a cyclist sweating more and beginning to sweat sooner, a process known as acclimatization. It can take up to ten days to acclimatize completely, though most of the process will have taken place within a week. Having achieved acclimatization, a cyclist must be aware that he or she now needs to continue drinking earlier and drink more fluids than usual.

Clothing

Those cycling in the heat must ensure they wear clothing that is made from textures that facilitate moisture wicking.

Dehydration

A fall in performance can begin with a loss of just 2 per cent of body-weight through sweat loss. As the body becomes more and more dehydrated, the core temperature begins to rise. This is the temperature in the parts of the body containing the vital organs, i.e. the brain, heart, lungs and kidneys. It is the temperature at which most of the metabolic processes going on in the body work most efficiently. The core temperature normally remains between 36.5 and 37.5°C. However, it may not necessarily be the same as the rest of the body. For instance, heat is generated during exercise and muscle temperature may rise to 39–40°C, though the optimal temperature for skeletal muscle functioning is 38.5°C.

If sweat losses are not replaced, the plasma volume drops, which causes the heart rate to increase as it tries to maintain cardiac output (i.e. the amount of blood pumped out by one heartbeat). Blood flow to the exercising muscles is maintained at the expense of blood flow to the skin. This leads to a drop in sweat rate and a rise in body temperature, which affects performance and can lead to fatigue, particularly on a hot day. A loss of just 2 per cent in body-weight can impair cycling performance and lead to premature tiredness. Cyclists may become aware of how much harder cycling is getting and that they are beginning to tire earlier than they expected. Alternatively, they may unknowingly reduce their self-selected pace. These effects can happen at various levels of dehydration and increase as dehydration increases. Dehydration does not just affect physical performance; it also has considerable impact on mental functioning, such as decision-making, reaction times, concentration, anticipation and skill delivery. Task inaccuracies also start to creep in too. Other consequences of dehydration that might be experienced by a cyclist include nausea and vomiting, feeling fatigued, developing a headache and muscle cramps. Research carried out at the University of Connecticut and published in 2012 also shows that even mild dehydration can alter mood and perceived energy levels. Mild dehydration in women can lead to headaches, fatigue and difficulty in concentrating, whilst men tend to report an increase in symptoms of tension, fatigue and anxiety (*see* Chapter 4 References, 2). Dehydration cannot be tolerated, mainly because the body cannot get used to it.

Assessing hydration status

Cyclists should work out their own fluid requirements and not just apply general guidelines. Knowing how much sweat is likely to be lost during training sessions of different types, duration and intensity, and in different weather conditions, will help a cyclist to estimate how much they need to drink to minimize dehydration. Simple but effective ways to establish hydration status include weighing every day, estimating fluid losses during different exercise sessions (cycle rides, weight sessions, running, etc.) and keeping alert to any changes in urinating habits. Body-weight should be recorded first thing in the morning – before breakfast but after a successful visit to the lavatory and ideally in a naked state. The same reliable scales should be used each time and ideally they should weigh to the nearest 100g. By recording daily weights in this way a cyclist will be able to track hydration status. A cyclist who is well hydrated will be able to maintain a stable body-weight which varies by no more than 0.5kg a day. A greater reduction than this from one day to the next will therefore almost certainly be the result of a fall in body fluid levels the day before, unless the cyclist is concurrently trying to lose weight.

If practical, weighing before and after a variety of training cycle rides can also help a cyclist work out the different fluid requirements for each type of ride. Acute changes in body-weight will be almost completely the result of the loss of body water. Depletion of glycogen stores and respiratory losses will be small in comparison to losses through sweating. Weighing should be done naked after a quick towel down to remove all traces of sweat. Ideally the weighing conditions post-cycling should be as close as possible to those pre-cycling. It is important to take into account the fluids and any foods consumed during the ride. To ensure the readings are as accurate as possible, trips to the lavatory should be made before the pre-cycle weighing and after the post-cycle weighing. Any losses of this nature that might occur during the cycle ride will of course skew the results somewhat and it will probably be necessary to do a re-run.

Sweat losses will continue for some time after the cycle ride has finished and there may also be urine losses too. Though a cyclist may be dehydrated, waste products still need to be excreted from the body. This explains the general advice to drink 1.5 litres of fluid for every kg body-weight lost as it helps to ensure the cyclist is fully hydrated. Calculating sweat losses during different types of cycle ride can be very useful in helping a cyclist to maintain good hydration status on any ride. Variations include duration, terrain and weather conditions.

Example of how to estimate sweat loss

Weight before cycling = 60kg

Weight after cycling = 58.5kg

Weight of fluid consumed while cycling = 1 litre equivalent to 1kg

Duration of cycle ride = 2 hours

Total sweat loss = 60 − 58.5 + 1 = 2.5kg

Sweat rate = $\frac{2.5}{2}$ = 1.25 litres per hour

As levels of dehydration increase, urine colour becomes darker and both the volume and frequency of needing to urinate decrease. By observing 'peeing' habits on a day-to-day basis, cyclists will know if they are becoming dehydrated and therefore will be in a position to rectify things before it is too late. Signs of being well-hydrated include passing urine frequently and in a reasonable quantity, and urine being pale in colour (first thing in the morning may be darker but it should be paler as the day goes on). Infrequent urination, small amounts and dark urine are the warning signs of a dehydrated body. A word of caution, though: cyclists who regularly use a multivitamin supplement will pass a slightly yellower urine than non-supplement users. This is because one of the B vitamins is yellow in colour and any excess to requirements will be excreted from the body in the urine. Vitamin supplement users should take this colour as their baseline and consider that any further darkening of their urine is probably due to dehydration. (There

are some other things that can affect the colour of urine, including eating beetroot, taking certain medications and illness.)

It is normal to urinate reasonable amounts anywhere between four and eight times in a twenty-four hour period. Females get the first urge to urinate when the bladder contains 200ml urine and they need to empty it when 400–500ml has collected. Men have different anatomy and tend to last longer before they need to urinate. Generally, urinating every two to four hours probably indicates enough fluids are being drunk.

Fluids before cycling

Anybody who cycles regularly must ensure that they have made up any fluid deficit before they cycle again. Beginning a cycle ride while still dehydrated from the previous ride could have a negative effect on performance. Perhaps replacing fluids after exercise should really be considered part of the preparation for the next exercise session. Some cyclists may consider hyper-hydration before exercise, but this is not a technique to be recommended as cyclists with a healthy pair of kidneys will just excrete any excess fluid. The position stand on exercise and fluid replacement published in 2007 by the American College of Sports Medicine recommends that 'Prehydrating with beverages, if needed, should be initiated at least several hours before the exercise task to enable fluid absorption and allow urine output to return toward normal levels.' Drinks containing sodium and/or salty snacks or small meals with beverages are also recommended as they can help in stimulating thirst and retaining the fluids that have been drunk. A cyclist who does not produce urine or who does produce urine but it is dark or concentrated should try to drink more – slowly but regularly. Drinking during several hours before cycling will allow enough time for urine output to get back to normal and leave the cyclist feeling comfortable and not worrying about being 'caught short' once off on the cycle ride.

A good protocol to follow is to start hydrating the day before, rather than leaving it until just before starting to ride. A low-intensity ride of about half an hour before a long road race will stimulate blood flow to the kidneys and create the need to urinate just before a race or hard training ride. After about fifteen to thirty minutes the blood flow to the kidneys will reduce and urine production will fall. This is the point at which drinking can begin in order to replace sweat losses.

Fluids while cycling

Some cyclists worry about the possibility of experiencing gastro-intestinal problems if they drink fluids while they are cycling. Others worry that they will lose pace while taking fluids at stations along the course and then drinking as they ride. Cyclists need to weigh up the positives of fluid intake against the potential loss in time. The need to drink while cycling will be somewhat dictated by the duration of the ride, the weather conditions and the work intensity involved – in other words is it flat-out racing or a more leisurely Sunday-afternoon-with-the-family pace? The current American College of Sports Medicine position stand on exercise and fluid replacement concludes that 'The goal of drinking during exercise is to prevent excessive (>2% body-weight loss from water deficit) dehydration and excessive changes in electrolyte balance from compromising performance and health.' The ACSM draws the further conclusion that

The need to drink while cycling will be dictated to an extent by the duration of the ride.

since there is a lot of individual variation in both rate of sweating and electrolyte content of sweat, fluid replacement strategies should be designed for individuals. In other words 'a one size fits all' strategy is not recommended!

For cycle rides lasting less than forty-five minutes in temperate conditions there may be little need to take on board fluids. However, the author suggests that it is a good idea to get into the habit of taking fluid bottles on all rides. The weather conditions can change, making the going harder, or the duration of the ride may be longer than anticipated for reasons beyond the control of the cyclist – such as road works, diversions, road accidents, flooding or just a flock of sheep blocking the lane!

The merits of keeping up fluid intake during training

Maximizes performance.

Contributes to ensuring a good recovery after training and races.

Helps prevent muscle cramps and reduce risk of some injuries.

Helps to avoid injuries as a result of poor decision-making caused by dehydration.

Rehydrating after exercise

Regardless of how much fluid has been drunk during training or competition, it is unlikely that all the losses have been replaced, and in any case sweating continues for some time after exercise

has ceased. A cyclist's aim should be to replace fluid losses and restore fluid balance after every race and every training session, either out on the bike or in the gym – indeed, after any form of physical activity that has induced sweating. Poor rehydration after exercise can have a negative effect on the next training session, particularly if it takes place in less than twenty-four hours and certainly if it has been a morning session to be followed by another session in the afternoon. Rehydrating becomes more and more crucial the less time there is between training sessions or races.

The generally accepted advice is to drink 125–150 per cent of estimated fluid losses in the first four to six hours after exercise. This takes into account the continuing loss of fluid through sweating which occurs for some time after exercise has stopped. There will be further losses as the body continues to produce urine, even in a dehydrated state, to get rid of waste products from the various metabolic processes going on in the body. The *Oxford Dictionary of Sports Science and Medicine* defines metabolism as 'The sum total of all the chemical reactions which take place in the body to sustain life.'

Plain water is not the best drink to have post-exercise as it does not restore fluid balance as quickly as other drinks. This can be crucial to cyclists who need to restore fluid balance as quickly as possible because they are training or competing again later in the day.

Until recently most research in

hydration post-exercise has been concerned with sodium and its role in helping the body to retain ingested fluid, and the fact that it is the most abundant electrolyte lost in sweat. Sports drinks containing sodium only seem to keep the body in positive fluid balance for one or two hours after exercise has finished. Increasing the amount of sodium would probably make the drink unpalatable and would also lead to greater losses of sodium in urine. Recent and continuing research looking at milk and liquid meals suggests that these drinks help the body to retain fluid and maintain a positive fluid balance for three or four hours after exercise. The effectiveness of sodium and carbohydrate to rehydrate is well understood and accepted. However, a drink consumed in the recovery period that contains fluid, electrolytes, carbohydrate and protein may become the drink of choice as it can rehydrate, restore glycogen levels and aid protein synthesis. Once fluids have been taken on board, a cyclist should find that the idea of consuming solid food becomes much more appealing.

It is important to recognize that the overall aim of fluid intake is to maintain a good hydration status as much as possible during exercise (cycling, running or gym work-outs). It is also important to accept that a more realistic goal is simply to minimize dehydration as much as possible, and to remember that over-hydration can produce negative consequences.

Top tips to help maintain a good hydration status

- Start all training sessions and races well hydrated.
- Replace sweat losses; rate of sweating depends on work rate, environmental temperature, humidity and clothing.
- Use a sports drink in training and races even if weather conditions are cold and wet.
- Take enough water bottles for the race and planned training sessions.
- Remember that thirst is not a good indicator of dehydration.
- Rehydrate as soon as possible after all training sessions and races.
- Monitor urine colour at all times.
- Drink a variety of drinks during the day – water (tap or bottled), juice, squash, tea, coffee, even the occasional soft canned drink.
- Carry a water bottle around at all times (work, college, out and about, etc.).
- Before cycling, heavy salt sweaters should consume a salty snack or add salt to their last meal.

Sports drinks

Sports drinks (commercial or home-made) are designed to give the correct balance of fluid and carbohydrate so that they empty from the stomach quickly, are absorbed rapidly in the small intestine and in doing so can play an important part in

Factors affecting rate of stomach emptying

Volume: high volume speeds up emptying

Fat: high-fat content slows down emptying

Osmolality: hypertonic drinks slow down emptying (more concentrated)

pH: low pH drinks slow emptying (more acidic)

Calorie content: highly calorific drinks slow emptying

Carbohydrate content: >8 per cent slows emptying

Type of carbohydrate: no effect

Type of exercise: no effect

Exercise intensity: 0–70 per cent VO_{2MAX} no effect

<75 per cent VO_{2MAX} slows emptying

Dehydration: slows emptying during exercise

minimizing dehydration and maintaining performance. However, some drinks that a cyclist might choose to drink can slow stomach emptying or delay the absorption across the wall of the small intestine. Either factor can delay fluid getting into the circulation and carbohydrate getting to the tiring muscles.

Commercial sports drinks do have science behind them in terms of their formulation and a major benefit they also offer is the consistency of their composition, unlike home-made drinks, which can vary quite considerably. Home-made drinks work out much cheaper but they tend to be less convenient.

Sports drinks can be used before and during exercise, but they can also be used as a recovery drink. Drinking a sports drink before training or a race helps to maintain good hydration status and top up muscle glycogen levels, and the sodium content helps to minimize urine losses before starting to cycle. During cycling sports drinks can help to maintain fluid and fuel levels, although water is usually enough on short rides in cool conditions. Recovery after cycling can be optimized by using a sports drink to replace fluid lost through sweating and initiating the process of replacing muscle glycogen stores. An aggressive recovery plan is particularly vital when a cyclist is going to be undertaking more exercise the same day.

A potential downside to a heavy reliance on sports drinks is that the boredom factor may creep in. Changing the brand of drink (with a similar composition of course) might help but in terms of using a sports drink in recovery, cyclists should consider having a pint of skimmed milk and a banana! This is something that is becoming a popular post-exercise choice among top cyclists – with good reason!

Cyclists should consider using sports drinks rather than water during intense exercise, exercise lasting more than sixty minutes or if they are a particularly salty sweater. However, it is important to start using a sports drink in all types of training where sweating is at least moderate. Water can be the fluid of choice in a light training session in temperate conditions, though there is a school of thought that a sports drink should be used in all exercise sessions. This way a cyclist will get used to drinking it and in light exercise probably will not drink much anyway. However, these drinks are called 'sports drinks' for a reason and they should not be used for social drinking or at non-exercise times, when a variety of other drinks can be taken, such as water, tea, coffee, hot chocolate, etc.

Home-made sports drinks

Though less convenient, home-made sports drinks work out cheaper but this must be weighed against the advantages of using a commercial sports drink. The concentration of commercial drinks will be accurate and consistent, and the well-known brands have very similar compositions based on research carried out over years, if not decades. The main reasons to buy sports drinks are convenience and reliability in the composition of the drink.

Sports drinks and tooth care

Dentists find two major problems with sports drinks: decay and erosion of the teeth. Decay is caused by dental plaque (a thin layer of bacteria). Plaque sticks to the teeth and breaks down sugars into acids, which then attack the teeth. Dental erosion happens when acid from the diet or regurgitation attacks the surface of the teeth. The main sources of acid in the diet are citrus fruits, fruit juice, soft drinks generally, pickled foods, vinegar or vinegary foods and sports drinks. Care must be taken to minimize the risks of dental decay and erosion as much as possible while still gaining the benefits of using sports drinks appropriately.

Minimizing dental problems

- Sports drinks should be drunk quickly – no sipping or holding/swishing in the mouth.
- The drink should be squirted behind the teeth and swallowed quickly – taking care not to choke.
- Cool drinks help to reduce erosion – though it may not always be possible to keep drinks cool.
- Teeth should not be cleaned for at least an hour after drinking a sports drink; a mouth wash should be used instead.
- Keep sports drinks for training and races only.
- Acidic drinks during the day should be avoided or limited.
- Nothing other than water should be drunk once teeth have been cleaned at bed-time.
- Floss and brush with desensitizing fluoride toothpaste twice a day.
- Have regular check-ups with a dentist and hygienist.

Case Study 3: Gail

For me, the exact science side of nutrition and eating on the bike doesn't do it for me. I find working out the correct weight and type of carbohydrates to be consumed per hour on the bike a bit boring. I know it's like using a power meter on the bike, making sure you cycle at the correct effort for the entire distance, but I'd rather go on 'feel', with a dash of logic thrown in, to make sure I don't bonk on the bike, which is when you grind to a halt because your energy levels are depleted. If it tastes good and gives me energy then I'm more likely to consume it in the right quantities. It's probably a bit too casual but I try to avoid an obsessive approach.

I tend to cycle in the morning and if I am going out on a reasonably fast, Surrey Hills ride of 50–60 miles of hilly undulation, I will have a pain au chocolate – high in calories and carbs – and perhaps an energy drink at least half an hour before I set off. Sometimes I will have a bowl of porridge but this tends to be the instant, just add hot water type, incredibly lazy and not as nutritious but easy to prepare at 7am on a Saturday morning. It can be difficult as you're not immediately hungry when you wake up but if you skip breakfast and just hop on the bike, you'll pay for it an hour into the ride. When I finally stagger back through the front door, four hours later, I look forward to something on toast – eggs, kippers or cheese – as a post-ride snack and occasionally I'll reach for a chocolate milkshake as a recovery drink.

One of the reasons I run and cycle to the extent I do is so that I can enjoy my food both on and off the bike and not at the expense of an ever-expanding Lycra waistband. My casual nutrition approach is different when it comes to an ironman bike leg (112 miles after a swim warm-up of 2.4 miles) when I know that I am going to have to get off the bike and run a marathon. Then I need to make sure I have enough energy to finish – it's easier to take on calories/energy on the bike than on the run and I pretty much stick to a liquid-only strategy, drinking a bottle of energy drink, high in carbs, every hour whilst on the bike – usually between six and seven hours. If I had solids on the bike I would find it difficult to get off the bike and go straight into the run. It's nutrition for nutrition's sake and it's as disciplined as I get. This strategy means that I have enough energy and fluid to complete the run.

I have some friends who set an alarm on their watch to go off at set intervals to remind them when to drink, leaving nothing to chance.

However, if I am taking part in one of the many weekend sportives on offer then I tend to treat this more as a running buffet, eating all the sausage rolls and cake I can lay my hands on at the aid stations en route. I want to be able to enjoy the ride and tuck into some usually off-limits food and not feel guilty. There needs to be some balance between just filling up the tank and also enjoying what's going in. I have a very sweet tooth so all the gels, chews and bars designed for the weekend warrior suit me. I think it's important not to get too hung up on what you have, just tweak things a bit to see what works for you. Too much sugar, though, can lead to peaks and troughs of energy levels and you may well crash and burn so balance your intake with some honest carbohydrates like bread and pastry. There is a container nicknamed a 'bento box' which sits on the top tube and provides easy access for gels, mobile phone, whatever, and I once saw a chap at an ironman race with his holder filled with boiled new potatoes. Whilst you can store energy bars and the like in your cycle jersey pockets, there's something convenient about having it right there in front of you, as a constant reminder to eat.

Last May I took part in the Rat Race's London to Edinburgh, 450 miles, two-day ride. Fantastic, it was an opportunity to eat my way from England to Scotland and take in some stunning scenery along the way. When you're resigned to the fact you'll be in the saddle for up to fifteen hours a day, you know you are going to have to have a constant energy supply (and a good supply of chamois cream), otherwise it's like setting off from London to Edinburgh with half a tank of petrol and expecting the car to go all the way – you need to make regular petrol stops. The aid stations were at most 50 miles apart and usually about 35 miles, which meant that roughly every two hours or so you had another cake, biscuit, flapjack or sandwich to look forward to. It's constant, full-on grazing and you never feel too full to cycle but you also ensure you won't bonk. At the overnight stop in York I had a fish and chip supper because I knew that this would help me with the following day's push to Edinburgh, even though when I got off the bike at 9pm I really just felt like falling asleep and by then my stomach had started to shut down; all that cycling and it's had enough. The next day was a similar smorgasbord of food and when I finally arrived at Holyrood Park, I was sure I couldn't have done it without that battered cod the night before.

@Norsemouse

CHAPTER 5

COMPETITION

Cycling competitions include road racing (the original cycle race), track riding, mountain biking and BMX racing (a type of off-road bicycle racing). The format of BMX was derived from motocross racing, with sprint races on purpose-built off-road single-lap race tracks. Road racing started in Europe towards the end of the nineteenth century and originally it was mainly the upper classes who took to their bicycles. However, the sport soon spread, appealing to people from all walks of life. The focus is now very much on endurance, mirroring the popularity of road running and marathons.

2012 Olympic road races

Women's distance – 140.3km

Men's distance – 250km

Women's race won in 3:35:21

Men's race won in 5:45:57

Between 1958 and 1993 the highlight of the British cycling calendar was the Milk Race, and in 2013 the race returned. It comprises a number of day races in several different locations. The best-known race, however, has to be the Tour de France, which is described as a multiple consecutive ultra-endurance event raced over twenty-one days and covering a distance of approximately 4,000 kilometres. The 2014 race took place between 5 and 27 July, with twenty-one stages and a total distance of 3,656km (2,272 miles). The winner of the race is the rider with the lowest cumulative time; almost unbelievably, the winning margin can be less than sixty seconds. During this event there is only one rest day.

Stage races can last from four to ten days with a daily programme including a mass-start road race, individual time-trials and team time trials. Daily stages can vary from prologue individual time trials of approximately 15 kilometres to 250 kilometre mass-start road races. An example is the Paris to Nice race.

Single-day events include mass-start road races such as the World Championship, Olympic Games road races and Paris–Roubaix race. These events cover a wide range of distances, from 60 to 250 kilometres and last anything between two and eight hours. Individual time trials on the World Championship and Olympic programmes for women are staged over 20–30 kilometres in times of thirty to fifty minutes and for men over 40–50 kilometres in times of forty to sixty minutes.

. . . .

Tour de France

This is an extreme endurance event, presenting different physiological demands at each stage. Not only is the sheer distance covered in the number of days amazing, but equally incredible is the energy expenditure, which can be up to 8,300kcal per day during the long stages. Over the whole race an average of 5,700kcal per day is expended and the food and fluids consumed on a daily basis must match this expenditure. If this were not enough, climatic changes over the duration of the race can be considerable too. Amazingly, several studies have shown that typical changes in body-weight over the whole Tour de France are only in the order of a loss of about 1kg. A study carried out during the 1989 Tour de France showed that cyclists consumed 49 per cent of their total daily energy intake and approximately 60 per cent of their total carbohydrate intake while they were actually cycling. This was achieved by the use of sports drinks, concentrated carbohydrate drinks and sweet cakes at a rate of 94g of carbohydrate per hour and approximately 4½ litres during each daily stage. Ten years later, however, another study showed a different eating pattern, although the actual intakes of energy and fuel were similar. Much more emphasis was placed on breakfast (the pre-race meal) and the post-race recovery meal. This was a substantial meal an hour after finishing the race, and supper some three to four hours post-race. In both studies high-carbohydrate intake was achieved by the use of biscuits, cake and confectionery, as well as bread, pasta, rice and sports foods. Approximately 60 per cent of energy intake came from carbohydrate, 15 per cent from protein and 23 per cent from fat. Over 49 per cent of the total energy consumption actually happened between meals. Approximately 30 per cent of the total daily energy was consumed as carbohydrate-containing drinks, establishing that fluids really are the easiest way to meet requirements. Studies have shown that the use of carbohydrate-containing drinks (as well as freely available

The physiological demands of the Tour de France are immense.

and suitable foods) can help maintain energy balance, which results in improved performance compared to using only water. Fluids are easier to digest and absorb than food, added to which hunger is suppressed during intensive physical activity, making the role of fluids even more important. Team doctors monitor the hydration status of the riders throughout the race, weighing them daily and monitoring urine for signs of dehydration. A positive hydration strategy can help in preventing under-performance and weight loss.

Consuming the required quantity of energy and nutrients can be a big challenge for a Tour de France cyclist. Carbohydrate-rich foods are bulky and often quite dry. Attempts are made to provide some more exciting but suitable foods into the day's menu. These include pancakes, sweets, marshmallows and wine gums. One Tour de France team is noted for taking 9kg wine gums to the Tour! Extra carbohydrate can be hidden by the addition of maltodextrin, a polysaccharide produced from starch by a process of partial hydrolysis. Maltodextrin is easily digested and is absorbed rapidly as glucose. It can be almost flavourless or moderately sweet, and can therefore be added to tea, coffee and other foods without affecting the overall taste.

Tour de France cyclists can be vulnerable to gut problems for a variety of reasons, including picking up contaminants from the road. Gut health is taken very seriously and items such as

Example day's menu for a Tour de France rider

On waking:
A juice drink to start hydration.

Breakfast:
A choice of porridge, rice, pasta, scrambled eggs, omelette, probiotic drink, yoghurt, bread, soft cheese, jams, honey and olive oil.

On the way to the start:
CNP energy and protein bars, flapjacks and Gatorade.

Race food and drinks:
CNP energy and flapjack bars, CNP gels with and without caffeine, small paninis filled with soft cheese, ham or jam, home-made rice cakes.
Water or carbohydrate electrolyte drinks.

Post-race:
CNP recovery drink and, on the bus, fresh cooked rice, boiled potatoes, tinned tuna, olive oil, honey, agave nectar.

Evening meal:
Starter – including some salad.
Main course – chicken, fish or red meat; rice, pasta and potatoes; and a choice of vegetables.
Dessert – fruit yoghurts and cake or fruit-based flan.

Before bed:
Either cereals with milk, yoghurt and honey or a CNP protein peptide shake.

vegetable juices, bio-active yoghurts, fish and olive oils and rice cakes are included in the daily diet. Sleep is also a crucial factor in maintaining performance across the whole race. Milky drinks before bed, an emphasis on not over-eating in the evening and avoidance of caffeine after 4.00pm are considered important strategies to help ensure a good sleep pattern throughout the entire race.

. . . .

Road racing

Road racing is an endurance sport requiring aerobic conditioning, a high power-to-weight ratio that translates into a cyclist being strong but light in weight. Specific nutritional concerns include providing enough fuel for racing and for maximizing recovery after the race has finished. The biggest dietary demand will therefore be for carbohydrate in order to maintain blood glucose levels, provide fuel for the brain and, crucially, fuel for the working muscles.

Days before the race

The key considerations before race day are to ensure adequate stores of fuel in the muscles. Carbohydrate loading should be something to consider before endurance and ultra-distance cycling races. Loading requires the cyclist to consume high-carbohydrate foods and fluids in the days leading up to the race to maximize the stores of glycogen in the muscles. Carbohydrate loading first became popular towards the end of the 1960s. Two separate groups of researchers, Ahlborg *et al.* and Bergstrom *et al.*, showed that following exercise and a very low carbohydrate diet, which had more or less totally depleted muscle glycogen stores, a diet containing 70 per cent carbohydrate consumed for three or more days could increase muscle glycogen stores significantly. Those subjects starting with low levels of muscle glycogen had an average time to exhaustion of 57 minutes; when a high-carbohydrate diet (averaging 600g per day) was consumed for a number of days, the average time to exhaustion increased to 167 minutes.

Such a carbohydrate-loading regimen would not apply to cyclists at the highest level, as professional cyclists and top amateurs compete too often to make it a viable option. However, studies have shown that individuals consuming 12–13g carbohydrate per kg body-weight per day did increase their stores of muscle glycogen compared to those consuming 9g carbohydrate per kg body-weight per day.

In recent years a more modified form of carbohydrate loading has become popular, particularly amongst highly trained athletes. This method requires a gradual taper in training in the week before a race but particularly in the last three days. At the same time the carbohydrate content of the diet has to be increased with the aim of achieving an intake of 8–10g per kg body-weight per day in the last three days, or in some individuals even the last five days, in order to maximize muscle glycogen stores. Generally in the days leading up to a race it is advisable to cut back on dietary fibre intake, mainly by avoiding high-fibre foods, in order to prevent gastro-intestinal problems. This applies particularly to cyclists who tend to suffer from pre-race nerves, which can sometimes lead to unwelcome and potentially embarrassing gastro-intestinal problems. (It was in a different sport but most people remember the problems that Paula Radcliffe quite literally ran into during a marathon.)

Along with the increase in carbohydrate, it is important to maintain a plentiful intake of fluids during the days leading up to the race. This is particularly important if high sweat losses are anticipated because of the expected weather conditions. In hot and/or humid weather conditions all cyclists, but particularly high salt sweaters, should consider adding salt to their food as well.

Pre-race nutrition

The aim of the pre-race meal is to make sure that muscle glycogen stores have been fully restored since the last training session. In the case of a race scheduled to start in the morning, it is the liver glycogen stores that need to be restored following the night's fast. Foods high in dietary fibre should be avoided on the day of a race and probably the day before the race too. Some cyclists may need to cut out high-fibre foods for a few days before a race in order to reduce the risk of encountering gastro-intestinal problems on and during race day. Foods high in protein and fat should be avoided as they can slow down the rate of gastric emptying, which can also lead to gastro-intestinal discomfort. The key nutrient to concentrate on before the race starts is carbohydrate, particularly in races lasting longer than sixty minutes and especially those taking place in the morning after the overnight fast. The pre-race intake of carbohydrate should be in the order of 1g per kg body-weight for races that take less than sixty minutes and between 1 and 4g per kg body-weight for longer races.

Of equal importance is the need for the rider to be well hydrated at the start of the race, which can be achieved by drinking plenty of fluids starting from the day before. This is important for all cyclists but especially for those cycling in hot and/or humid conditions, and those who have been cycling the day or days before. Whatever a cyclist chooses to eat at their pre-race meal, it should leave them feeling comfortable and with no signs of gastro-intestinal problems, other than perhaps some pre-race nerves. There is a maxim that sports dietitians and nutritionists are fond of, which is that nothing should be done (in this case eaten or drunk) that has not been tried and tested in training. Some cyclists may have specific foods that they like to have pre-race, perhaps as some form of psychological boost or just as a particular superstition they have acquired. This is understandable but it does carry the potential risk of problems, such as what happens if that particular item is not available, as could be the case if the night before the race has to be spent away from home. Something so simple can have quite a negative effect on a cyclist, particularly one who is pinning their hopes on a good result.

Suitable pre-event meals

Breakfasts:

Low fibre cereal or porridge with skimmed or semi-skimmed milk and sliced banana and honey or sugar

Crumpets, muffins, bagels or bread/toast with low-fat spread and honey, jam or marmalade

Pancakes with golden syrup or honey and sliced banana

Low-fat milk shakes or smoothies

Meal replacements (Build-Up or Complan) are an ideal choice for cyclists who struggle with breakfast on race days (or any other day!)

Baked beans on toast (though the fibre content may be too high for some cyclists)

Spaghetti in tomato sauce on toast

Baked potatoes with low-fat fillings

Filled rolls, bagels or sandwiches (using chicken, tuna, low-fat cheese or honey for fillings)

During the race

Taking carbohydrate on board during a race can help both the muscles and the nervous system. Unlike most other sports, it is possible to take on board fluids and food while racing, though this requires practice in training, using the same fluid bottle, drink and food that will be used in the race. 'Carrying' fluids and suitable food items during long rides should not normally present any problems, certainly compared to a distance runner, who literally does have to carry everything. Suitable items can be carried on the bike frame or in jersey pockets. Cyclists are less likely than distance runners to encounter

Solid foods should be eaten early on in the race.

gastro-intestinal problems as there is less bounce.

The amount of carbohydrate required depends on the rider and the intensity of the race. A general recommendation would be to aim for between 40 and 90g carbohydrate per hour. The maximum amount of glucose that can be absorbed in an hour is 60g. Using a mixture of glucose and fructose, this figure can be increased to 90g per hour. This is particularly beneficial during events lasting more than two hours. Regularly using carbohydrate in training has been shown to train the gut to absorb carbohydrate at a faster rate. Further research has shown that receptors in the mouth detect carbohydrate, which in turn energizes the brain. This could be of value to cyclists competing in shorter events.

Whatever a cyclist decides to eat must have been tried and tested in training rides over a similar distance and terrain. A cyclist should not be tempted by seeing what other cyclists are doing and certainly should never do something for the first time in a race. It must be affordable and travel well, be easy to consume while cycling and, just as importantly, be enjoyable while cycling. What tastes great at home in front of the television may not be so tasty while cycling hard and fast out in the wind and rain!

Solid foods should be eaten early on in the race, switching later to simple carbohydrate sources such as gels.

The risk of becoming dehydrated is reduced in races taking place in

Possible suitable items for during a race

SMALL sandwiches – jam or honey

Energy and sports bars

Bananas (large)

Flapjacks, Buzz bars, cereal bars and granola bars

Fruit loaf, cake and cookies

Dried fruit (particularly larger fruit such as apricots)

Jelly babies and similar jelly sweets

Chocolate (though it is high in fat and melts in heat)

Sports drinks

Fruit juice

Soft drinks and de-fizzed cola

Sports gels (with the appropriate amount of water)

cool conditions (less than 25°C) and lasting less than sixty minutes, although there will be a lot of variation between cyclists. This is another reason why it is so important that cyclists have a good idea of what their likely sweat losses are in different races, different weather conditions and over different terrains. Having this information can help a cyclist to have at least a good idea of how much fluid and what type of fluid to drink in different weather conditions and different races. In a study published in 1995 cyclists improved their performance in a laboratory-based time trial when it was undertaken after they had cycled for one hour followed by a large fluid replacement, compared with when they had cycled for one hour followed by only a small fluid intake (Below et al., 1995).

Many cyclists consider water as the fluid of choice, perhaps flavoured with their favourite squash. However, sports drinks provide not just water, but carbohydrate and sodium as well. These drinks help to maintain blood sugar levels and replace sodium, as well as maintain a good hydration status. Using a sports drink rather than water could help in improving overall performance – perhaps the difference between coming first or second!

Recovery

A well-planned recovery strategy is important at any time but is absolutely essential when a cyclist is competing over one or more days. There has to be complete recovery (or as near complete as possible) on a daily basis. No matter how hard a cyclist tries to maintain fluid and fuel levels during the race, there will be a need to restock the muscles with carbohydrate and restore the body to a fully hydrated state. What is required is no different from the recovery strategy after training or the recovery strategy after a single-day event. The difficulty is repeating it day after day despite accumulating tiredness, both physical and mental. As the event continues, it is also quite likely that some minor injuries may need attention too.

A final word – alcohol

Though usually associated with team sports, drinking alcohol post-competition does occur in other sports, under the guise of celebrating or perhaps just commiserating. It is standard medical practice to treat soft tissue damage (muscles, tendons, fascia, ligaments and skin) with vasoconstriction or RICE techniques (rest, ice, compression and elevation). Alcohol is a particularly good vasodilator, particularly of the blood vessels to the skin, and it is possible that drinking large quantities of alcohol may lead to further swelling at the site of the injury. As a result, recovery might not be so speedy. Abstaining from alcohol for twenty-four hours (at least!) would appear to be sound advice for an injured cyclist to follow, particularly one keen to get back on the bike as soon as possible.

Case Study 4: Mark

My nutrition for everyday cycling would generally consist of balancing and increasing my daily intake of carbohydrates, proteins and fats to prevent catabolism due to the increased activity levels that I would be undertaking. I have found through trial and error that a balance of 65 per cent carbohydrate, 15 per cent protein and 20 per cent fat works best for me. I would work out my daily kilocalorie requirement based on the reduced body-weight that I want to be during the event; to do this I use the Schofield Equation. This is a method of estimating my total energy intake requirement based on my basal metabolic rate (BMR) as I find this most accurate.

My daily intake of food would usually consist of an early breakfast of porridge with mixed berries or a banana (I sometimes change this for muesli), and to drink a Berocca vitamin and mineral effervescent tablet diluted in water. I would then snack on seeds and nuts throughout the morning. Approximately two hours before my bike ride I will then eat a balanced meal, usually chicken or fish with dark green vegetables and sweet potato. I will eat again approximately thirty minutes before the ride and this usually consists of a small snack of possibly fruit or a cereal bar. During the ride I will fill one water bottle with water and the other with SIS GO Electrolyte sports drink for energy and hydration. I alternate between these two water bottles for the duration of the ride. If the ride is to take longer than two hours then I take with me quick-release energy gels. After the initial two hours I would take an energy gel for each additional hour of my ride. Immediately after my ride I drink a pint of milk and eat a portion or two of fruit (I used to use post-workout protein shakes but I seem to get the same benefit from milk and fruit, as well as it being far cheaper). In the afternoon I snack on fruit and raw vegetables leading up to my evening meal, consisting of a pasta or rice-based dish with protein being either fish or white meat. I only eat after this if I have not made up my daily quota of kilocalories.

Eight days prior to an event is when I start my carbohydrate loading, with the event being on the eighth day. I start by decreasing my carb intake to 50 per cent, with 25 per cent protein and 25 per cent fat, whilst still cycling at high intensity for a long period of time for three days. On the fourth day I decrease my cycling intensity by half and increase my carb intake to 70 per cent, with 15 per cent protein and 15 per cent fat. Finally, to max out my glycogen stores, on the fifth to the seventh day I do very little or no cycling, and increase my carb intake to 75 per cent, with 10 per cent protein and 15 per cent fat.

On the day of the event I eat my normal breakfast two hours before the event and set up my water bottles the same as my normal rides. I take energy gels one every two hours on the ride. If it is a very long event so that you have fuel stations and you can re-fill your water bottles, I take a re-sealable sandwich bag with a portion of my SIS GO electrolyte in it. Some fuel stations do provide energy drinks but I have found that not all energy drinks agree with my stomach and some can give you a bad headache, which is not what you want on a long event.

CHAPTER 6

SUPPLEMENTS AND ERGOGENIC AIDS

The European Food Safety Authority (EFSA) defines a food supplement as 'a concentrated source of nutrients or other substances with a nutritional or physiological effect whose purpose is to supplement the normal diet. They are marketed in dose form i.e. pills, tablets, capsules or liquids in measured doses, etc.' The EFSA also states that 'Supplements may be used to correct nutritional deficiencies or maintain an adequate intake of certain nutrients. However, in some cases excessive intake of vitamins and minerals may be harmful or cause unwanted side-effects; therefore, maximum levels are necessary to ensure their safe use in food supplements.'
The *Oxford Dictionary of Sports Science and Medicine* defines an ergogenic aid as 'Any factor which improves athletic performance above normal expectation. Ergogenic aids are frequently thought of as drugs only, but they could also be psychological techniques (such as hypnosis), mental practice and suggestion, music, oxygen and nutritional substances.'

Sports foods and drinks

Sports foods and drinks such as bars, gels, sports drinks and recovery drinks do supply nutrients in a convenient way but ordinary food such as bananas, cereal bars, flapjacks and so on can do the same job and probably at a much lower price! It is not difficult to produce home-made sports drinks (*see* Chapter 4) but popular sports drinks such as Gatorade, Lucozade Sport and Powerade do provide an easy to use, standard formulation that can help to make a busy, hectic lifestyle a little more manageable. For the travelling cyclist, whether holidaying or competing, commercial sports drinks in powder form may be considered an essential item to include when packing, along with gels and sports bars. It should go without saying that anything packed must have been used (and enjoyed) when cycling back home.

Energy drinks

Energy drinks should not be confused with sports drinks such as Gatorade, Lucozade Sport or Powerade, which all help to maintain a good hydration status during exercise as well as topping-up energy levels and replacing sodium lost in sweat. Energy drinks have higher carbohydrate (sugar) contents than sports drinks, which can actually hinder and slow the rate of absorption of fluid. They should therefore not be the drink of choice before, during or after exercise, when the aim is to replace fluid lost through sweating. Energy drinks can be potentially dangerous in large amounts if drunk with other stimulants or with alcohol. If all this were not reason enough to avoid using energy drinks, it should be pointed out that most are also not tested for purity or contamination. Drinking an energy drink could potentially result in a positive drug test.

Nutritional supplements

What is a supplement? A supplement to what? Fundamentally it is a supplement to the diet, so it makes sense to work at getting the diet right first and then perhaps there will be no need for a supplement at all! Nigel Mitchell, the Head of Nutrition at British Cycling/ Team Sky, believes that riders should get the basics right rather than just focusing on supplements. He compares this to making a cake: 'A rider needs to ensure the cake is right before adding the icing and sprinkles.' The International Olympic Committee (IOC) produced a Consensus Statement on Sports Nutrition in 2010 which stated that 'The use of supplements does not compensate for poor food choices and an inadequate diet, but supplements that provide essential nutrients may be a short-term option when food intake or food choices are restricted due to travel or other factors.'

However, there is no additional benefit to taking a multivitamin and mineral supplement on a regular basis if a cyclist is enjoying a diet that already provides all the essential nutrients. The problem is that many people (not just cyclists) are not sure that their diet does always provide all the essential nutrients. For them, the

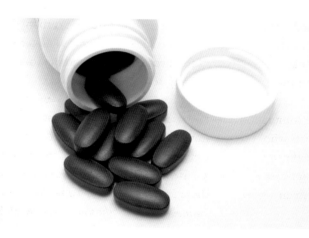

Mineral supplements can be considered a nutritional insurance policy.

supplement is rather like a nutritional insurance policy. A cyclist may make the decision to take a multivitamin and mineral supplement because of a lifestyle issue. Work, cycling and social events may make for a hectic way of life and a diet somewhat limited in variety and quality, mainly because of tight time constraints. A daily vitamin and mineral supplement does what it says on the label – it supplements the (less than adequate) diet. Care should be taken to read the label before buying. Cyclists should buy only supplements that contain no more than 100 per cent of the Recommended Daily Amount (RDA) of vitamins and minerals in the recommended dosage (usually one tablet a day).

Many athletes take supplements for bone and joint health because of the impact that their particular sport has on their joints. For instance, running can put a strain on the hip, knee and ankle joints. These supplements usually contain glucosamine, chondroitin and the long-chain marine sources of omega-3 fatty acids (fish oils), which are all known to help keep joints supple and flexible. Cyclists who include running in their fitness programme but do not look after their joints could be laying the foundation for problems later in life. Cyclists who have a family history of osteoarthritis may like to consider using a joint care supplement, as could those with an aversion to eating oily fish!

Hard training can lead to an increased risk of picking up a minor infection or illness, which could result in lost training time or, worse, having to pull out of a race. This is because hard training can weaken the body's immune system, while high levels of stress hormones reduce the body's ability to fight any resulting infection. The main culprit is cortisol, a stress hormone released during heavy training sessions. Cortisol helps the body to use fat and protein as energy sources when glucose supplies are low, but it also suppresses phagocytes – cells that are capable of engulfing and digesting particles and other cells. There are several supplements marketed with the claim that they boost the immune system and increase the body's ability to fight infections. These include Echinacea, colostrum, zinc and glutamine, but strong evidence that they do have this ability is sadly lacking. Strategies that are known to help include incorporating well-timed rest periods into training programmes, ensuring energy intake matches energy requirements (i.e. no unintended weight loss) and making sure that carbohydrate intake matches requirements in terms of frequency, intensity and duration of training sessions over the week. Taking in carbohydrate during prolonged exercise also reduces the release of stress hormones. Probiotics (classed as food supplements) contain what are known as 'friendly' bacteria – two examples of these are *Lactobacillus acidophilus* and *Bifidobacterium bifidum*. These work by modifying the gut microflora population and this in turn influences immune function in a positive way! Cyclists who regularly succumb to gastro-intestinal problems should consider using food products containing these probiotics in their regular diet. Examples of such products are the Actimel or Yakult ranges.

Supplements to help performance (ergogenics)

With so many supplements available in health food shops, specialist sports shops and, of course, on the internet, how can cyclists know if a supplement will actually do what it says in the advertisement? The advice is to apply the author's SMART rule.

The SMART rule

Safe: Is it safe from a health point of view? Does it definitely, without any doubt whatsoever, *not* contain any banned substance?

Moonshine: Is the 'science' relating to it rubbish or is it accepted scientific fact?

Appropriate: Is it really going to be of benefit to a cyclist?

Realistic: Is the dosage and formulation appropriate for a cyclist?

Tested: Are the claims backed up by research, or is the evidence all anecdotal, or relying on celebrity endorsements?

Any supplement a cyclist might consider using must be safe and legal, must not compromise health and certainly must not contain any substance that appears on the WADA Prohibited List (www.ukad. org.uk/resources/documents/2014-prohibited list).

Creatine

Creatine occurs naturally in the body and the highest concentration is found in skeletal muscle. When the body is at rest, the amount of creatine (as creatine phosphate) is three or four times the amount of adenosine triphosphate (ATP), the immediate energy source for muscle contraction. In healthy people muscle creatine is broken down to creatinine and excreted in urine, approximately 2g a day in total. The body makes creatine from amino acids in the liver but creatine levels are also topped up by the diet, particularly one containing meat but also fish. A typical carnivorous diet will provide between 1 and 2g of creatine a day, but vegetarians will miss out on this dietary supply of creatine completely.

Creatine phosphate provides energy for high-intensity exercise and is particularly important in helping the body to recover between intense bursts of exercise such as sprints. Muscle fatigue is associated with a drop in ATP concentration. To avoid fatigue the rate of ATP regeneration has to match the breakdown of ATP as closely as possible. The use of creatine supplements can increase the amount of creatine and creatine phosphate stored in muscles. There is no shortage of studies showing that creatine loading can increase the amount of repeated high-intensity bursts of exercise that can be achieved when there is only a short recovery time (less than two minutes) between them. Cyclists completing single or multiple sprints might like to consider experimenting with creatine in training. However, supplementation may lead to weight gain, which could be a big minus for some cyclists.

The traditional method of taking creatine is to load with 20g creatine a day for four to five days. This is followed by a maintenance dose of 2–3g a day, which will maintain the high concentration of creatine for up to thirty-five days. If a maintenance dose is not taken, there will be a slow, gradual reduction in creatine concentration. It takes about four weeks for the body's creatine levels to return to their original resting levels. If a loading phase is not implemented, a maintenance dose of 2–3g a day can be taken for thirty days to maximize muscle creatine. Creatine uptake in the muscles can be improved by having a carbohydrate-rich meal or snack (50–100g carbohydrate) at the same time as taking the supplement. (*See* Chapter 3 for 50g portions of carbohydrate-containing foods.) It is worth noting that there is a lot of variation in how people respond to creatine supplementation, with some people appearing to be complete non-responders. Vegetarians have no dietary source of creatine and as a result have low muscle creatine concentrations. Perhaps as a way of compensation, they do show a greater response to supplementation than people who have gained a higher natural creatine concentration through regular inclusion of meat in their diet.

Creatine supplementation can cause an initial increase in body-weight of between 1 and 3kg. This usually occurs within the first few days of loading. Rather than being an increase in muscle, this is a result of water retention. Weight gain over the following weeks (usually about eight weeks) will be the result of the positive effect of creatine supplementation on training. Creatine is not on the WADA list of banned substances and a supplementation regime as suggested is considered to be generally safe. It is probably a good idea for cyclists who decide to try creatine supplementation to keep a diary, recording body-weight at the start of the loading phase and during the maintenance phase, as well as any benefits and/or side-effects that become apparent. Reassuringly, creatine supplementation does not appear to have any harmful effects on health. Over the years there have been anecdotal reports of muscle cramps, strains and tears, though this has not been validated in any creatine studies. There have also been publications suggesting that creatine supplementation could have detrimental effects on liver metabolism. In fact, creatine supplementation studies in humans, lasting up to five years, have not shown any significant rises in plasma urea or liver enzyme activity, which suggests that creatine does not present any health risks in healthy adults. That said, experts usually suggest that creatine should not be used chronically, nor should it be taken by anyone who has renal disease or could possibly be at risk of developing a kidney problem, such as diabetics or people with high blood pressure. As with all supplements, care must be taken to ensure that the product is pure and ideally that analytical tests have proven the product to be safe to use.

Caffeine

First, it is important to debunk the advice often given by pseudo-nutritionists and journalists that coffee should be avoided because of the dehydrating effects of caffeine, particularly in situations where fluid balance might be compromised. A review of current literature, published in 2003, looked at the effect of caffeine intake on fluid balance (R.J. Maughan, J. Griffin (2003), 'Caffeine ingestion and fluid balance: a review', *Journal of Human Nutrition*, 16: 411–20). The authors concluded that there was no support for the suggestion that drinking caffeine-containing drinks as part of a normal lifestyle led to fluid loss in excess of the volume actually drunk. In other words, caffeine did not have a diuretic effect, nor was it associated with poor hydration status. Drinking less than 300mg caffeine a day (from all sources) will not compromise hydration status. This amount of caffeine is roughly equivalent to three mugs of coffee or six cups of tea.

Caffeine is found in tea, coffee, cocoa, colas and other soft drinks, energy drinks and chocolate. It can also be found in some over-the-counter medications such as some cold and flu remedies, pain relief products, anti-histamine tablets and diuretics (substances that increase the elimination of fluid from the body through urination). Everyday sources of caffeine usually provide between 50 and 150mg

Caffeine is found in tea, coffee and cocoa.

caffeine but it is possible to buy products containing as much as 300–500mg per serving. Reports have suggested that as much as 90 per cent of the world's adult population consume caffeine in their everyday diet.

Caffeine content of a range of beverages

Average cup of instant coffee = 75mg*

Average mug of instant coffee = 100mg*

Average cup of brewed coffee = 100mg*

Average cup of tea = 50mg*

Regular cola drink = 11–70mg per can**

Regular cola drink = 16–106mg per 500ml bottle**

Regular energy drink = up to 80mg per can*

* Source: Food Standards Agency advice for pregnant women on caffeine consumption, 10 October 2001.

** Source: MAFF Food Safety Directorate, 1998.

Caffeine is readily absorbed after ingestion. Blood levels rise and peak after approximately sixty minutes. The half-life is reported to be between two and ten hours. This is the time it takes for half of any given amount of a substance – in this case caffeine – to have been broken down. The actual effects of caffeine may last anywhere from one to seven hours. However, for most people the half-life of caffeine is four to six hours. In other words, the highest concentration will be in the blood about an hour after consumption, and this level will have fallen by half some four to six hours after consumption.

Caffeine is not a nutrient but a pharmacological agent, as well as a socially acceptable drug that is weakly addictive. It is also one of the most widely used aids or support in everyday life and sport, and has been shown to improve performance over different distances and a variety of cycling events. From 1980 to 2003 a caffeine level in urine above 12mg/litre was not permitted in any sporting competition and such a level would result in a positive doping test. The intention was to deter athletes from consuming large amounts of caffeine, often as much as 500mg in a very short space of time. Caffeine may be a weakly addictive drug but it is also a widely acceptable one, and it would be difficult to control its consumption. Also, although difficult, it would not be impossible to go over the limit with a normal diet. As a result the World Anti-Doping Agency (WADA), which provides resources to sporting organizations, decided to take caffeine off the list of banned substances. This took effect from January 2004, although the use of caffeine is still monitored.

There is good evidence to show that caffeine can exert an ergogenic effect, particularly in events lasting more than one minute. Positive effects of caffeine can be seen on exercise capacity in submaximal exercise lasting less than ninety minutes, in sustained high-intensity exercise lasting between twenty and sixty minutes, and in short-duration supra-maximal exercise lasting between one and five minutes. A caffeine intake of just 1.5mg per kg body-weight forty-five to sixty minutes before the start of exercise improves performance compared to a placebo. (The *Oxford Dictionary of Sports Science and Medicine* defines a placebo as 'a substance or situation that should not have a beneficial effect on performance but they may do so, possibly as a result of suggestion, but for no other known biological or physical explanations. The placebo effect is well established and is used as an ergogenic aid.') Larger doses of caffeine do not seem to be any more effective.

Ingestion of caffeine during exercise lasting more than sixty minutes has also been shown to improve performance, although the ergogenic effect of caffeine in high-intensity exercise lasting less than one minute is less obvious. Perhaps the most significant effect of caffeine is its action as an adenosine antagonist. The *Oxford Dictionary of Sports Science and Medicine* defines an antagonist as 'a drug that occupies a receptor site without producing a response, but which prevents the action of the endogenous substances or an agonist drug'. Raised levels of adenosine reduce the arousal level and help induce sleep instead. Caffeine works at reversing this desire to fall asleep. Anyone who has burnt the midnight oil revising for exams will probably have experienced how helpful mugs of black

coffee can be in keeping awake when other students are sleeping! Caffeine also appears to lower the perception of effort during exercise, as well as decreasing the awareness of muscle pain. The positive effects of caffeine on performance are experienced by people who drink caffeine-containing drinks on a regular basis, as well as those who do not. In fact, the responses generally are very variable and are not necessarily related to the amount of caffeine consumed normally on a regular basis.

People respond differently to caffeine, with some experiencing side-effects such as anxiety, jitteriness, headaches, abdominal discomfort, muscle tremors and impaired coordination with high doses of caffeine. Many people do use coffee to help them stay awake, but insomnia – either having difficulty falling asleep or staying asleep – is definitely not a good preparation for an important race. On the other hand, when sleep has been disturbed or compromised in some way, drinking a caffeine-containing drink could help to restore performance.

Caffeine is a mild diuretic. Although its use has been discouraged in the past, small to moderate intakes of caffeine appear to have little effect on urine losses or general hydration status in those who drink caffeine-containing drinks on a regular/daily basis. Cutting back on the habitual intake of coffee, tea and colas would probably result in an overall reduced daily intake of fluids, which is definitely not a desirable outcome!

Caffeine induces mild dependency and if regular caffeine consumption ceases abruptly, symptoms such as headaches (and in someone particularly sensitive to caffeine a migraine attack), irritability, fatigue, poor concentration and a reduction in mental performance can occur. Individuals may also feel sleepy and yet find they cannot actually fall asleep. These symptoms usually appear twelve to twenty-four hours after caffeine withdrawal, peaking about forty-eight hours after withdrawal and lasting for anything from one to five days. Strangely the timing is not particularly linked to the amount of caffeine consumed.

People respond differently to caffeine intake and to the withdrawal of caffeine from the diet, and those differences can be enormous. Having a frequent high intake of caffeine can cause rapid desensitization in some people and they will need to ingest even higher doses to obtain the same result. Cyclists who decide to use caffeine in races should reduce their intake in the days leading up to the race, although there is no good evidence to suggest that complete withdrawal of caffeine is required.

Energy expenditure may be increased by the use of caffeine, though only very slightly. This is because caffeine stimulates the basal metabolic rate – the amount of energy needed when the body is fasting and at complete rest. It is unlikely that even people with a very high caffeine intake would gain weight when they stopped using caffeine-containing drinks.

If they did, it would most probably be due to the drinks they were having instead – unless, of course, they were only drinking water!

Buffering agents (e.g. sodium bicarbonate alias baking powder)

Buffering agents can help in high-intensity exercise lasting from about one minute to ten minutes but are of no benefit in exercise lasting less or more than this. The major potential side-effect (and this could be a deciding factor) is diarrhoea. It is therefore vital to try out the use of a buffering agent in training before attempting to use it in a race.

During this type and duration of exercise, the muscles start producing lactate and hydrogen ions, which results in an acidic environment – which can be both good and bad! Good because it provides the necessary energy for the hard exercise but bad because it also causes pain and disrupts muscle function. To counter the acidic environment that has been created, an alkaline substance is required. Sodium bicarbonate works on an acidic stomach and can do the same with muscles. The usual dose is 0.2–0.3g sodium bicarbonate per kg body-weight, consumed ninety minutes before the event. This regime should be tried out in training first as there is a potential risk of experiencing a gastro-intestinal upset. Sodium citrate can be used instead of bicarbonate but it is not thought to be as effective.

Cyclists not enthusiastic about using sodium bicarbonate or sodium citrate could try an alternative way to overcome the problem by using a β-alanine supplement. This has to be taken over a period of four to ten weeks, following the dosage advised on the packaging. It works by increasing the amount of carnosine, an important buffer, in muscles. The *Oxford Dictionary of Sports Science and Medicine* defines buffers as 'chemical substances that resist abrupt and large changes in hydrogen ion concentration of the body fluids on addition of an acid or an alkali'.

Beta-alanine is an amino acid and the precursor of carnosine, an important buffer found in muscle. It helps the body to handle acidic build-up in muscle and could therefore be useful in maximizing performance over short distances, such as 4km pursuits, or may help with sprint finishes in longer events.

Nitrates

Nitrates are naturally occurring substances that the body can convert into nitric acid. The most popular source of nitrates in the sporting world is beetroot juice, but beware – it makes urine turn pink or even red! Short-term supplementation can help to reduce the amount of oxygen needed for a specific amount of work – in other words, it helps to reduce the energy cost of exercise, which in turn could mean cycling faster in events lasting a few minutes or longer. It also reduces blood pressure and increases blood flow. Studies using beetroot juice or sodium citrate, with doses ranging from 300 to 600mg nitrate taken in either a single bolus or for as many as fifteen days, have shown significant moderate benefits on performance for time to exhaustion tests. A study by N.M. Cermak, M.J. Gibala and L.J.C. van Loon published in the *International Journal of Sport Nutrition and Exercise Metabolism* (2012, 22: 64–71) showed that six days of nitrate supplementation in the form of 0.5 litre beetroot juice a day reduced pulmonary oxygen uptake (VO_2) during submaximal exercise and improved time-trial performance in trained cyclists. A scholarly review by P.M. Christensen, M. Nyberg and J. Bangsbo, published in the *Scandinavian Journal of Medicine and Science in Sports* (Vol. 23, Issue 1: e21–e31, Feb, 2013), examined the effect of nitrate supplementation on exercise performance. This was carried out through a systematic review and meta-analysis of controlled human studies and the conclusion was that 'despite not reaching statistical significance, the small positive effect on time trial or graded exercise performance may be meaningful in an elite sport context'. However, the authors also suggested that more data are needed so that the effect of nitrate supplementation on exercise performance can be better understood, giving an insight into the best ways of supplementing with nitrate. In seventeen studies reviewed, beetroot juice and sodium nitrate were the most commonly used supplements in doses ranging from 300 to 600mg nitrate given in a variety of ways from a single bolus to fifteen days of regular ingestion.

Supplements for muscle gain

Protein supplements, amino acid supplements and protein bars are the biggest sellers among sports nutrition products generally. Cyclists do have an increased requirement for protein compared to less active people but this does not mean that requirements cannot be met without the regular use of these products. For most cyclists it should be quite easy to get enough protein from an all-round healthy diet and, though it may appear convenient to use a protein supplement, it is worth checking on the label to see what is actually in these supplements! The main ingredient in many protein supplements is whey protein, a high-quality protein found in milk. (The other milk protein is casein.) In recent years more and more athletes from a wide range of sports have been drinking (and enjoying) 'real' milk, rather than using the protein supplements based on milk. Perhaps it is worth mentioning that between 1958 and 1993 the Milk Race was considered the most prestigious cycling event in the British calendar.

It was called this because the Milk Marketing Board (now disbanded) was its sponsor and to this day this sponsorship remains the longest association that the sport has ever had. The main reason to include whey protein is obviously to help repair and build muscles, which in turn helps the body to adapt to training and enables a cyclist to train harder. However, recent research has suggested it can also help in weight management, as well as improving body composition.

Whey provides a source of leucine and other essential amino acids; very usefully, it is readily digested. Of course, in many situations the option to 'drink milk' may not be a practical or viable one. For cyclists who can see a benefit in using a whey protein powder, the best advice would be to choose a simple product rather than an expensive one claiming special manufacturing techniques or extra (unnecessary) ingredients. A serving providing 20–30g of whey protein would be sufficient to meet the protein requirements at a single meal or snack.

Amino acids

Amino acids are the building blocks of protein, or in simple terms the ingredients that go to make a particular protein. Including good-quality protein in the daily diet in sufficient amounts to meet protein requirements is not difficult in countries where food is plentiful.

Consuming individual amino acids on top of this is unnecessary and expensive, and remember they do have an energy (calorie) value!

Herbal supplements

Many health food shops sell herbal supplements that are claimed to boost testosterone levels, the assumption being that this will have a positive effect on muscle strength, power and size. To date, studies in humans have not shown this to be the case, and such claims are based solely on test-tube studies in the laboratory. Cyclists should steer well clear of these supplements (no pun intended!).

. . . .

Banned substances

Substances can be banned from competition for a number of reasons. The substance might give a cyclist an unfair advantage over other competitors; it might be dangerous; there may be ethical issues; or it may simply be illegal. It is important that cyclists remember that the list does not just cover performance-enhancing drugs but also simple cold medications.

Walking into any health food or sports shop, a cyclist will be amazed at the number of products claiming to lower body fat and increase muscle mass. Be aware that any product that actually does this will be on the banned substances

list; worse, it may be linked with serious health risks, or both. Weight-loss products have been shown to contain ingredients that are on the banned substances list, as have over-the-counter (OTC) products such as decongestants. If they are used, and the cyclist happens to be drug-tested, the result would be a failed drug test. Cyclists must be aware of the strict liability principle: in other words, the cyclist is responsible for everything that he or she consumes, and ignorance is no defence for a failed drug test. Perhaps competing cyclists should adopt the attitude that anything they ingest (other than 'proper' food and drink) is banned unless they have first cleared its use with an expert such as a club doctor, sports dietitian or club physiotherapist. Both UK Sport and the English Institute of Sport (EIS) provide advice on this subject on their websites in the 'Useful Information' sections.

The Prohibited List World Anti-Doping Code (WADA)

This is a list that is produced annually and comes into effect on 1 January each year. It contains lists of substances and methods that are prohibited at all times (both in and out of competition), which are anabolic agents, peptide hormones, growth factors and related substances, beta-2 agonists, hormone and metabolic modulators, diuretics and other masking agents, manipulation of blood and blood components, chemical and physical manipulation, and gene doping. Substances and methods prohibited in competition are stimulants, narcotics, cannabinoids and glucocorticosteroids. Some substances are prohibited in particular sports but none is specified for cycling. As a matter of interest, alcohol is prohibited in competition only in aeronautic events, archery, automobile racing, karate, motorcycling and powerboating. Unless otherwise stated, beta-blockers are prohibited in competition only in archery, automobile racing, billiards, darts, golf, shooting and skiing.

Perhaps the simplest option is to assume that a substance is banned until it has been checked out by a GP or by the appropriate Cycling Federation; in the United Kingdom this would be either British Cycling (www.britishcycling.org.uk/insightzone) or UK Anti-Doping (UKAD) (www.ukad.org.uk). UKAD particularly supports national governing bodies of sports to ensure their athletes are clean and stay clean. At an individual level, they can support athletes applying for Therapeutic Use Exemption (TUE). A cyclist who has a particular illness or condition may need to take a regular medication which is included on the Prohibited List. A TUE would authorize that cyclist to take the medicine (www.wada-ama.org/en/science-medicine/tue).

CHAPTER 7

THE TRAVELLING CYCLIST

Cyclists who ride or compete only in their own country should find much of the information they need to keep their bodies fit and healthy, to provide enough fuel for cycling and to maintain good hydration status at all times (or as close to all times as possible), in the previous chapters. However, what is missing when travelling is the easy access to food that is normally in the fridge, freezer or kitchen cupboard at home. Even short trips can present a cyclist with a dietary dilemma of what to eat and drink, particularly if travelling to compete in a race.

Nevertheless many cyclists do travel abroad, perhaps for a cycling holiday or to compete in a race. In such cases normal home-based routines can become disrupted, the food may not be palatable, favourite sports drinks may be unavailable, or weather conditions may vary from what was predicted. Before leaving home for a cycling holiday or a race abroad, it is a good idea to do some research into predicted weather conditions for the time of year in the particular country or countries to be visited. Hot and humid conditions mean that even more care is needed to maintain a good hydration status at all times. Care should also be taken to wear cycling kit appropriate for the conditions. Even the best cyclists can get this wrong. Chris Froome wore a mesh jersey while training in South Africa during the month of January and, because such tops cannot reflect the sun, sun creams are vital. Unfortunately he did not use enough and ended up with a rather burnt back. Food may be unfamiliar or just not to a cyclist's taste. Poor food intake could lead to a lack of energy, resulting in a significant fall in cycling performance. The first thing to consider is a dietary plan to cover travel from home to the final destination.

· · · · · · · · · · · · ·

Travel at home

It is well established that one should never do something before, during or after competition that has not been tried out and practised in training. In this case, a cyclist should only eat and drink what they are used to having in training, and certainly should not be tempted by any food that might be on offer at the race. Invariably such food is aimed more at spectators than competitors anyway!

Suitable food items for travelling to races from home

Fresh fruit, especially bananas

Dried fruit

Cereal bars, muesli bars and flapjacks

Sandwiches, rolls or bagels with low-fat fillings

Fruit buns and scones

Pretzels, Snack-a-Jacks and Twiglets

Low-fat milk shakes

Water, fruit juice and sports drinks

Travel abroad

Travelling to another country can involve changes in time zones. It is generally considered to be easier travelling from west to east rather than from east to west. Crossing one or two time zones does not normally have any negative effects on travellers, but crossing three or four zones can and five or more zones will certainly take several days to adapt to. The symptoms of jet lag include disorientation, feeling less alert, light-headedness and bad temper. Energy levels may be low and there can be loss of appetite. Despite feeling tired during the day, it may be hard to sleep at night. Bowel habits may change and there may be an overall feeling of demotivation and general discomfort – just 'not feeling right'. It generally takes one day for each time zone crossed to feel 'normal' again. It is possible to pre-adapt a little by getting up and going to bed one or two hours earlier or later, depending on whether travel is eastward or westward. Watches should be set to the new time zone on arrival, and certainly must not be kept on 'home time'. Travelling can be very tiring, even though most of the time is spent sitting down, but bedtime should be as close as possible to the 'correct time' in the new time zone. A sleeping pill may help in adjusting the body's internal clock. Napping, particularly at the normal sleep time back home, should be avoided as this tends to keep the body in 'home time' rather than in 'new time'. Daylight inhibits the release of melatonin (a natural hormone that influences the body's biological clock) and this helps the body to adjust to the new environment. Use of melatonin should always be discussed in good time before travelling, ideally with a sports doctor or otherwise with a general practitioner. It is crucial to get the timing of dosing right. For an eastward flight this should be in the evening, and for a westward flight in the morning. Following a westward flight an early night for the first few days after arrival can help get over jet lag. After an eastward flight any exercise should be done in the evening rather than the morning. Some cyclists may wish to use caffeine in an attempt to overcome fatigue, albeit for only temporary relief. Caffeine should not be used late in the afternoon or in the early evening if an early bedtime is planned. There is some evidence to suggest that a meal containing carbohydrate can help with sleep. Insulin, a hormone secreted by special cells in the pancreas in response to raised blood glucose levels, allows tryptophan (an amino acid) to cross the blood-brain barrier where it is converted into serotonin, another hormone that encourages feelings of calm and happiness (sometimes referred to as the 'well-being' hormone).

Heat and/or humidity

Cycling in hot and/or humid conditions leads to an increase in sweat rate. Unless significantly more fluids are drunk than are normally consumed at home during a cycle ride, a cyclist will become dehydrated. As well as a fall-off in performance, there will be a greater risk of heat illnesses, the major ones being

heat cramps, heat exhaustion, exertion heat injury and heat stroke. Heat cramps are probably caused by an imbalance between body fluids and electrolytes such as sodium. Cyclists should acclimatize to the weather conditions before tackling long, hard rides and always ensure they hydrate well before, during and after cycling. They should also drink frequently, ideally using a sports drink containing water, salt and carbohydrate. Water alone is not good enough in these conditions. Cool drinks are generally more palatable, so it makes sense to use insulated drinks bottles if possible.

A cyclist suffering from heat exhaustion will have a weak but rapid pulse and low blood pressure – signs that may not be noticed by anybody, including the cyclist. Sometimes the cyclist may complain to other cyclists of a headache, dizziness or weakness. Sweating may be reduced but body temperature will not be raised to a dangerous level. However, exertion heat injury symptoms can point to something a lot more serious. Such symptoms include gooseflesh, chilliness, headache, weakness, dry skin, nausea, vomiting, unsteadiness, confusion and even unconsciousness. Immediate treatment is

Acclimatize to weather conditions before tackling long rides.

necessary; the cyclist should be helped to dismount and allowed to sit down in a cooler, shaded spot (if possible). Sponging with cool water or ice, drinking and using a fan if available are also all useful immediate treatments. Heat stroke is the most serious condition: left untreated, it can lead to death. Symptoms include mental confusion, convulsions and loss of consciousness. Sweating may stop and as a result the skin becomes dry and hot. Emergency treatment is essential, probably including an aggressive lowering of body temperature and obviously no more exercise – at all! An air-conditioned environment, a cool shower or ice bath and fans can all help to bring down the temperature and in some cases intravenous fluids will need to be administered.

Some cyclists find they lose their appetite in hot environments and as a result overall food intake drops to the point where daily energy requirements are no longer being met. Taste sensations can also change, which can make foods seem very monotonous and boring. This increases the risk that on a day-to-day basis energy requirements might not be met. Cyclists who do experience a loss in appetite in hot conditions must make an active effort initially to eat more than usual as this could help to reduce the risk of weight loss. Hydrating with sports drinks (made up from powder with clean water) rather than water alone will contribute to energy intake, as well as maximizing hydration status. However, a certain amount of caution is needed. The requirement for fluids may be so great that a reduction in overall energy intake from food will be required if an increase in body-weight is to be avoided.

Acclimatization

The body is able to adapt to heat and humidity by a process called acclimatization. It can take between one

Coping with heat and humidity
- Ensure good hydration by drinking before, during and after all cycling.
- Use sports drinks before, during and after cycling (chilled if possible).
- Increase fluid and salt intakes above normal. Achieve this by adding salt to meals at the table and also drinking with meals. However, care should be taken not to drink so much that not enough food is eaten at meal-times.
- Have a drink by the bed in case of waking up in the night.
- Wear light rather than dark coloured clothing.
- Ensure kit is not limiting the area of exposed skin – wear less if it is.
- Use a well-ventilated helmet.
- Cool the body, clothes or helmet with sponges or sprays.
- Use a sunscreen (but not a waterproof, non-breathing one).
- Keep hair short or off the neck. Shave off facial hair.

and two weeks before a cyclist becomes fully acclimatized and this should be borne in mind when planning a training programme or working out when to fly out for a race. Acclimatization is achieved by making blood flow to the skin more efficient, starting the sweating process earlier, increasing sweat output and making sweat less salty. Cyclists can begin the acclimatization process before leaving home by the use of saunas, steam baths and hot baths, as well as just piling on more clothes when cycling and, if appropriate, at other times too.

Training and competition in the cold

Cycling in cold weather conditions almost inevitably leads to a decrease in core body temperature and an increase in energy requirements. This means that cyclists riding in these conditions will need to up their intake of energy from food and fluids to match this increased requirement. Priority should be given to carbohydrate-rich foods and fluids because of the limited capacity of muscle to store carbohydrate (as muscle glycogen). However, dietary fat can help to increase energy intake as it is more energy dense on a weight basis than carbohydrate. Hot palatable food is essential when cycling in cold conditions, mainly from a psychological point of view. Hot food is associated with a warm sensation and a feeling of satisfying the appetite. It can also help keep up morale. In cold weather it is particularly important to maintain a regular food intake, both from meals and snacks or refuellers. Cyclists who feel the cold at night may find that a small meal or snack before bedtime helps to maintain body temperature. This in turn can help to prevent a sleepless night. Cyclists should pay attention to their fluid intake, as it is all too easy to make the assumption that sweat losses will not be so great compared to cycling in warmer weather. Cold weather conditions actually suppress the thirst sensation and therefore replacing

The core body temperature will drop when cycling in cold weather.

fluid losses will require an active effort. Try to keep to a schedule of regular drinking rather than leaving it to random hydrating. Fluid losses will still depend on exercise intensity, duration, environmental temperature and the clothing that a cyclist is wearing, both the type of clothing and the number of layers worn. Keeping a daily record of body-weight first thing in the morning, pre-cycling and immediately post-cycling, together with a diary of fluid intake, can help in minimizing dehydration and the negative effects it can have on cycling performance.

Altitude

Cycling at altitude presents a cyclist with several challenges, including hypoxia (a condition in which there is an inadequate supply of oxygen to the tissues), extremes of temperature and low humidity. Humidity is a measure of the content of water vapour in the atmosphere. For the cyclist the air will feel very dry and breathing will be harder. This will lead to more fluid being lost in breath than is lost when cycling at lower altitudes, which obviously increases the risk of a cyclist becoming dehydrated. There will also be an increase in insensible loss of water from the skin. Evaporation from the skin will also be more effective at altitude because of the drier nature of the air. Cyclists will therefore need to make a very big and conscious effort to increase fluid intake as soon as they arrive at altitude. Failure

to do this could lead to a loss in plasma volume (the fluid part of blood), which in turn leads to an increase in the viscosity or stickiness of the blood. This can have serious negative effects on cycling performance as aerobic exercise capacity is compromised. The heart has to work harder to pump the thicker blood around the body, and this adds further stress to the heart and blood circulation.

The body loses fluid at a much faster rate at altitude. Cyclists should start to monitor their fluid intake even before they arrive at their final altitude destination, and continue to monitor their intake for the whole altitude experience. Loss of appetite at altitude is not unusual. However, it is also one of the symptoms of acute mountain sickness, others being nausea, vomiting, headaches and dehydration. On recovery from mountain sickness, appetite may remain suppressed. This is in part because the taste sensation can also become depressed. Food can seem monotonous and not particularly appetizing. Cyclists who are already aware of these issues will know they have to work actively at increasing their food intake if weight loss is to be avoided, or at least minimized as far as possible. Loss of body-weight as lean tissue (muscle) and body fat can have disastrous effects on cycling performance. It is therefore advisable to acclimatize and only undertake gentle exercise (of any type) on arrival at altitude. This is important at any time but particularly prior to any competitive cycling. At altitude, energy requirements increase by at least 10 per cent compared to requirements at sea level. A healthy intake of carbohydrate-rich foods and fluids is particularly vital as carbohydrate is very much the preferred energy source at altitude. Aggressive refuelling after every cycling session is essential too. Oxidative damage during cycling may be greater at altitude than back home and an increase in fruit and vegetable intake could certainly help to ensure the diet contains plenty of essential antioxidants. One of the adaptive responses of the body to altitude exposure is an increase in red blood cell production. A good iron status is therefore crucial. Sensible actions before leaving for altitude would be to have a haemoglobin check at the GP surgery, as well as ensuring the diet contains plenty of iron-rich foods and vitamin C (see Chapter 1).

Eating away from home (and avoiding stomach upsets)

Cycling in foreign countries can increase the risk of suffering an upset stomach unless special attention is paid to where meals are eaten and what is actually eaten. This is not the time or place to start experimenting with unusual foods, even if they are the speciality of the country. At the very worst, this could lead to being unable to compete in a race or having a very miserable holiday, particularly if it is a family cycling holiday.

Cyclists who suspect that food might be an issue in the country they will be cycling in should consider taking some suitable, portable food supplies from home. It is always a good idea to check with the airline first to make sure that no items will be confiscated on arrival at the final destination – that would be really annoying, and not a good start to the preparations for a race or the family cycling holiday!

Suitable items to take abroad

Breakfast cereal

Dried milk

Cereal bars, energy bars, sports bars

Savoury biscuits, rice cakes, pretzels

Trail mix with dried fruit, nuts and seeds

Peanut butter, jam, honey

Meal replacements

Sports drink powder

Competing cyclists or families enjoying a cycling holiday in their home country should not encounter any food or nutrition problems, whether they are staying in a bed and breakfast, guest house or hotel. However, it is a good idea to check meal-times when booking, particularly breakfast and the last sitting for the evening meal. If an evening meal is not provided, care should be taken when choosing where and what to eat.

Fast food outlets

The best choice is a basic beefburger with lettuce and tomatoes but no other trimmings, and a milk shake of any flavour, including chocolate. Adding cheese adds extra fat. Chicken burgers are often coated with mayonnaise, deep fried and served with more mayonnaise, so are not as healthy as they might sound. French fries (thin chips) absorb more fat in cooking than thick ones. Perhaps fast food outlets should be the last choice, when nothing else is open!

Chinese food

Chinese cooking uses a lot of vegetables and not much fat, apart from the obvious deep-fried items such as sweet and sour pork, which should of course be avoided. Most menus give descriptions of the ingredients in a dish and how it is cooked, but if in doubt it makes sense to ask the waiter rather than hazarding a guess. Soups and crispy duck are better choices than spare ribs or spring rolls. Ideal main courses are stir-fries or steamed dishes with plain boiled rice or noodles. Cyclists who tend to overeat when eating out might like to try using chopsticks rather than a knife and fork. It slows down the eating rate and perhaps helps prevent eating too much!

French or Italian food

Good starter choices are bread and breadsticks with a non-creamy vegetable soup such as minestrone. Starters to avoid include whitebait and, sadly, garlic bread. Creamy sauces should also be declined. Meat, fish and poultry should be steamed, poached, baked, casseroled or roasted rather than fried, battered, creamed, buttered, sautéed or 'au gratin'. Bulk up on boiled or mashed potatoes, pasta or rice. Vegetables that have been fried, roasted or tossed in butter are not such good choices as simple steamed or boiled ones.

Greek food

Greek meals are built around salad vegetables, bread, pasta and rice, though they can contain quite large amounts of olive oil. Olive oil is considered the healthiest of all the oils but it is still advisable to be careful how much is eaten as the calorie value is no different from other oils – high! Tzatziki (yoghurt with cucumber and garlic) with pitta bread or stuffed vine leaves are good starter choices. Salads can be served without dressings but with feta cheese as it is a low-fat variety of cheese. Greek meals usually contain a range of grilled meats and fish, and cyclists who are still hungry can enjoy Greek yoghurt with fresh fruit and honey. Greeks do like their food, so be aware of the portion sizes!

Indian food

Indian menus usually explain what each dish contains and sometimes how it is cooked. Samosas, crispy rolls and other fried starters should be avoided. However, tandoori dishes and kebabs are not served swimming in oil or ghee (clarified butter with the water and salt removed). Other good nutritional choices include biryani, dhansak, rogan josh and jalfrezi, all served with plain rice, naan, chapattis, roti or paratha. Main courses to avoid are kormas, pasandas and masalas (all served in creamy sauces), anything cooked in ghee and special fried rice. Puddings are also not good choices but fruit and ice-cream should satisfy any sweet-toothed cyclists who are still hungry after their curry.

Mexican food

Enchiladas and burritos are good choices as long as care is taken not to eat too much cheese and sour cream. The same applies to guacamole, which should be enjoyed in small amounts only. Fajitas – grilled meat served on a flour or corn tortilla – are a good option. Rice can be used to bulk up the carbohydrate intake. The 'not so good' choices include corn chips, deep-fried potato skins and tostadas.

Pizza

Here the best choices are deep pan pizzas, choosing from ham and pineapple, margherita, vegetarian or seafood, and avoiding if possible salami and pepperoni pizzas. It is probably a good idea to decline any offers of extra cheese on any pizza, just to help keep the overall fat content down.

Traditional pubs

Good choices for pub meals include jacket potatoes with baked beans, chilli or tuna, and shepherd's pie with vegetables. A Ploughman's with a little more bread and a little less cheese, soups with bread and sandwiches, filled rolls or French sticks are also all good options. Less good will be most savoury bar snacks and anything fried, as they will all lead to high intake of fat, something cyclists following the advice in this book will not be used to!

Case Study 5: Phil

Phil started cycling in 2005, having previously played squash. He joined a local club and in the last three years took his cycling more seriously, having coaching and making his training a lot more specific.

Training
During the winter Phil puts in lots of miles. He trains between twenty and twenty-five hours a week, taking one day off each week. He checks his resting pulse and heart rate to ensure he is remaining in good health and that there are no signs of any illness.

During the racing season his cycling is much more specific, including hill sprints, standing sprints and shorter distances, with a total training time of ten to fifteen hours a week.

Competition
Racing is usually two or three times a week with short, hard circuit races lasting an hour during the week and longer races up to 80 miles at the weekends. He tries to peak for races like the premier calendar and competes in France three times a year. There are always big races at Easter and at the end of September. Fortunately Phil is good at peaking for these important races.

Fluid intake
During training Phil drinks two 500ml bottles, one containing water and the other originally CNP but now he uses NWN (a new company).

Racing
Two hours before a race Phil eats some rice or pasta with chicken. Races start very early so this may mean eating between 5.00 and 6.00am.

For races over 70 miles Phil drinks two or three bottles of energy product with a flat coke handed up to him towards the end of a race. If the race is over 80 miles he will also eat something. This is usually a CNP bar or a Power bar. He also uses gels, taking one every thirty minutes, and for circuit races he has one before. These tend to be SIS GO gels. Later on he uses CNP energy gels.

After the race Phil uses CNP Recovery straight away followed by 'ordinary' food such as sandwiches about an hour later. However, he does find eating quite difficult after a hard race.

Supplement use
Phil takes beetroot juice three days before an event and multivitamins and omega-3 fatty acids on a regular basis. To help protect against colds (he works in a pub when not cycling) he takes vitamin C and Echinacea.

CHAPTER 8

SPECIAL CONSIDERATIONS

Previous chapters contain information that is relevant to all cyclists but certain population groups of cyclists may need to carry out some fine tuning to meet specific and individual requirements. There may be a need to reduce body fat and body-weight – perhaps this is the reason for cycling in the first place. The specific nutritional requirements of children, veterans and females must be considered. Lifestyle choices such as becoming a vegetarian or vegan will also require particular care to ensure that all the essential nutrients are still being met by the diet. Events such as the Christmas and New Year period or summer holidays can play havoc with body fat levels unless an element of restraint is applied. It is still possible to enjoy these times without seeming a killjoy to the rest of the family and their friends.

Reducing body fat or body-weight

Obviously cycling, or indeed any form of exercise, can help in reducing body fat or body-weight but paying attention to diet can ensure a sensible and steady weight loss, which has no negative effects on cycling performance. Serious cyclists work hard to maintain low body fat levels in order to increase their power to weight (mass) ratio. Hill riders particularly tend to be smaller and lighter than other cyclists. A low body-weight and lean body will also be an advantage in any sport where the body has to be moved, marathon running being an excellent example. Unnecessary body fat is 'dead weight', which a cyclist has to move, using up more energy in the process. This can become a very important consideration where cycling over long distances comes into play, or over a particularly hilly ride. However, rapid weight or body fat loss does not equate with getting the maximum out of training or races. Genuine, long-lasting weight or body fat loss must be achieved slowly, frustrating though this might be, but as body-weight drops a cyclist should start to appreciate the benefits it brings. For serious competitive cyclists attempts to reduce body fat/body-weight should only be undertaken early in their preparation period. Attempting to drop body fat or body-weight at any other time could compromise performance, whether during a heavy training period or a race.

Measuring success

Ideally it is body fat that should be measured, rather than body-weight. Unfortunately most cyclists do not have access to getting this measured unless they belong to a gym or possibly a cycle club where skinfold thickness measurements can be taken at regular but not too frequent intervals. The skinfold method is probably accurate to plus or minus 4 per cent of the true body fat percentage. Using bathroom scales is a much cruder method of determining fatness or thinness, as it basically just gives an overall body-weight with no indication of any changes in body composition. It is worth remembering that a pound of body fat takes up more space than a pound of muscle, so as body fat reduces and muscle increases, the scales may not indicate a great loss but the looseness of clothing that was previously tight certainly will.

The mechanics of weight loss

For body-weight to remain the same, the body has to be in energy balance. When weight loss is the goal, energy consumed from food and drinks must be less than energy expended over a period of time. This means consuming less energy than the body needs to function and to meet the daily demands for energy, as well as the energy demands of cycling and any other physical activity that might

be undertaken, such as gym work-outs and weight sessions. It is sensible to aim for a steady weight loss of 1–2lb each week. A faster weight loss will result not only in body fat loss but possibly also in muscle loss, which is definitely not desirable. A pound of body fat is equivalent to 3,500kcals, so to lose a pound a week means an energy deficit of 500kcals a day. This can be achieved by reducing food intake and alcohol intake (if relevant) by 500kcal a day. It can also be achieved by expending an extra 500kcal a day in exercise over and above the normal activity expenditure cost. For many people employing a combination of both a reduction in food intake and an increase in exercise is the ideal – a case of spreading the hardship! Rapid weight loss might look encouraging on the bathroom scales, but unfortunately this will include not only the much desired body fat loss but also a loss of valuable muscle too.

What to avoid

Sadly there is no shortage of so-called experts happy to give out advice about how to lose weight; indeed, faddy diets have been around since Roman times. In October 2013 the British Dietetic Association offered advice on how to recognize bad dietary advice for weight loss. This included avoiding quick fix diets, anything suggesting magical fat-burning effects (notably grapefruit), avoidance of whole food groups, promoting one food (such as the cabbage soup diet), any diets claiming easy and rapid weight loss, eating foods in particular combinations, anything that sounds too good to be true and finally anything that does not include advice about physical activity.

How to lose weight

Following the advice in earlier chapters will help a cyclist make sensible food choices to support the increased requirements of cycling. Where there is a genuine need to lose weight, particular

General tips to encourage a steady but small weight loss

- Eat only when hungry.
- Always eat sitting down, ideally at a table.
- Do not eat whilst watching television or a DVD, in front of the computer or at the cinema – all idea of how much is being eaten is lost.
- Downsize plates and bowls to help control portion sizes.
- Eat slowly. People tend to eat less – possibly up to 15 per cent less when they do. Eating quickly does not allow the brain time to send messages that enough has been eaten. By the time the messages do come through, too much has already been consumed.
- Putting down cutlery between mouthfuls can help in eating more slowly and so reduce the risk of over-eating.
- Eat little and often. It takes less energy (calories) to digest one big meal than the same amount divided into two or three smaller ones.
- Do not cut out any meals, especially breakfast.
- Finish a mouthful before preparing the next one.
- Talk a lot. It is not polite to talk with a mouthful, though!

- It may help to keep a diary of everything eaten and drunk each day. This can shock people into realizing how much they do actually eat – and what they eat too.
- Weight or body fat loss does not happen at a steady rate each week. Do not give up if one week there is no loss – the next might be a 'double' loss.
- Do not miss out on refuelling immediately after cycling – this is very important. Don't wait for the next meal to eat – the refuelling process will be less efficient.
- Cut out snacking but don't confuse it with refuelling.
- Avoid crash diets, fads and pills, laxatives and diuretics.
- Drinking plenty of water in conjunction with a weight loss programme appears to help to reduce weight compared with just a weight loss programme.
- Don't focus on hunger but think about positive things like feeling healthier, cycling faster, and tackling hill climbs better.
- Tell family and friends about the plan and ask them for support and encouragement to help maintain progress towards the end goal.

attention must be paid to fat and alcohol intakes. These provide more calories on a weight basis than carbohydrate and protein. Arguably alcohol could be cut out of the diet completely, though perhaps cutting out for the first one or two weeks and then just drinking in a measured way occasionally is a more realistic, achievable target. Consideration must be given to maintaining carbohydrate intake as cutting back too drastically could have dire consequences for cycling performance. The limited stores of carbohydrate will start to run out sooner than other cyclists'. It will also be harder to concentrate, which could put the cyclist at greater risk of being involved in an accident. Low glycogen stores can also compromise the immune system.

Care is always needed to make sure that a cyclist does not lose sight of the essential need for good nutrition during an attempt to achieve lower body fat and body mass levels. Portion control is the key, not a reduction in the range and variety of foods eaten (apart from the high-fat ones).

Children

Even if children are cycling for fun on family outings, it is still important to consider and take into account the environmental conditions. Children are not necessarily as aware of the effects of the weather as adults and they need supervision, especially in relation to heat loss and the consequences of dehydration. They are not nearly as efficient as adults in adapting to extremes of environmental temperatures. They get hotter but sweat less and have a lower heart output and a greater surface area to body volume ratio. Compared to adults they are much less able to transfer heat from inside the body to the skin. They are also not very good at recognizing thirst, and therefore not good at responding to it either.

Generally children need between six and eight glasses of fluid a day, plus the water they get from the food they eat. Young children need smaller drinks (approx. 150ml serving) and older children need more (approx. 250–300ml serving). However, requirements will be higher for those taking part in any form of exercise, including cycling, particularly when the weather conditions are warm, hot and/or humid. It is a good idea to get a young cyclist to start drinking water during the hour before a long cycle ride. During such cycle rides children should be encouraged to drink every 15–20 minutes and certainly whenever they feel thirsty. As thirst is not a particularly good indicator of hydration status, it is much better to keep to a specific regime rather than wait for the cry 'Can we stop? I'm thirsty!' By this time the young cyclist has probably already become dehydrated. In many situations water will be sufficient, for instance on cycle rides lasting less than an hour in temperate weather conditions. However, a sports drink should be considered if the cycle ride is to last more than an hour, or if it is a particularly hot or humid day. A white residue visible on the cyclist's skin or clothing (particularly in the armpit or groin areas) is an indication of sodium losses as well as fluid. In this case a sports drink (commercial or home-made) would be a considerably better choice than just plain water. It is worth remembering that sugars found in soft drinks and sports drinks, together with the acids that are also present, can provide a wonderful environment to encourage acid production and growth of bacteria, which can then lead to dental caries. Damage limitation includes regular brushing of teeth, drinking water after eating, drinking sweetened drinks with a straw or squeeze bottle, and eating lots of milk and cheese (which contains casein). If children do not automatically drink immediately after the cycle ride finishes, they need to be reminded, especially if it has been hot or humid and sweat losses have been high.

Children who cycle regularly and are generally of a sporty nature will need more energy; in other words, they need to eat more than their less active friends. However, all children, whether active or not, need enough energy for growth and maturation, otherwise the result could be a delay in maturation and slow growth. For young cyclists this could also mean poor sporting performance. If this should happen, cycling intensity must be reduced and energy intake increased. During growth spurts or periods of intense physical activity, particular attention should be paid not just to energy intake but also to intakes of protein, calcium, iron and zinc. Flavoured drinks will probably be more popular than water. These should be used to help ensure an adequate fluid intake is achieved. This is particularly relevant in hard or long cycle rides or when cycling in weather conditions that lead to greater fluid losses, such as heat, humidity or both.

Females

Females differ from males in their metabolism and performance. They oxidize more fat than males at the same absolute and relative exercise intensities. Together with other physiological differences, it would seem that females are particularly suited to endurance and ultra-endurance events. Key nutritional areas that female cyclists need to address include overall energy intake, which can often be on the low side, nutrients involved in bone health (calcium, vitamin D and magnesium), and nutrients involved in energy production, specifically oxygen transport (iron, folate and vitamin B_{12}). Published data suggest that females tend to have the same calorie intake regardless of the intensity or duration of training sessions or competitions. Related to this, carbohydrate intake tends to be low, which can lead to an inability to keep up the required training load, along with mental and physical fatigue, increased risk of injury and illness and muscle protein breakdown. Female cyclists need to ensure an intake of 5–7g carbohydrate per kg body-weight per day when training lasts an hour a day. Intake needs to increase to 6–10g per kg body-weight per day for high-intensity training lasting four or five hours a day. Recommended protein requirements for females generally are 1.2–1.3g per kg body-weight per day, which should be achievable for all female cyclists, even vegetarians and those omitting red meat from their diet. However, this only holds true if overall energy intake meets daily requirements. Restriction of fat intake to lose weight or reduce body fat levels is common among female athletes. However, this weight loss is not always necessary or advisable. A low intake of fat may limit the absorption of fat-soluble vitamins and the intake of essential fatty acids may fall short of requirements. The macronutrients of most concern to female cyclists are calcium, iron, magnesium, zinc and B vitamins. Vitamin D can also be a problem for some female athletes. However, as this vitamin is made by the action of sunlight on the skin, female cyclists should be making more than enough without relying on dietary intake. The information provided in Chapter 1 highlights the major food sources for individual nutrients.

Many female cyclists work hard at reducing their body fat and certainly an excessive amount of body fat and a corresponding increased body-weight can make cycling much more of an effort.

However, care is needed to ensure that a female cyclist does not fall into the trap of reducing weight and body fat too much. Always feeling tired, being prone to bad temper and feeling stressed could all be signs that too much weight has been lost. Putting on a few pounds will not have a negative effect on cycling performance – probably the opposite in fact. Not only that, everyone, including family, friends, fellow cyclists and the cyclist herself, will feel much better and enjoy cycling much more.

Carbohydrate cravings

Women tend to report cravings more than men do, and research suggests that hormonal changes may be the reason. It certainly helps to explain the food cravings experienced during pregnancy and at different times of the menstrual cycle when the metabolic rate rises and there is a tendency to eat more. A similar thing can happen during times of stress. Serotonin, a chemical made in the brain, helps to create a happy, calm mood and carbohydrate-rich meals help to increase serotonin levels. People who try to follow low-carbohydrate/high-protein diets soon realize the role carbohydrate plays in the body as they become tired, lethargic and irritable. Female cyclists should already be including plenty of carbohydrate in their daily diet but here is yet another reason not to limit carbohydrate intake.

• • • • • • •
Masters

Ageing is not necessarily a reason for a loss in cycling performance. In fact, studies show that the causes are probably down to poor quality of training, less training and greater occurrence of injuries. Darrel Meard in the *Oxford Textbook of Sports Medicine* (1994) states that 'Age is not a barrier to performance, only an inconvenience.' For anybody contemplating taking up cycling in later life, certainly for those over fifty years old, it is probably advisable to have a general health check-up and if possible, and obviously if advised by the GP, to have an electrocardiogram during exercise. The main problems facing an older cyclist are that recovery takes longer than for younger cyclists, and it is much harder to regain previous fitness levels after a lay-off for health or other reasons. With increasing age there is a tendency for muscle mass to decrease and fat mass to increase. However, maintaining regular exercise through cycling will help to maintain muscle mass and reduce the risk of an increase in fat mass. It is important for older cyclists to concentrate on enjoying good-quality carbohydrate and protein generally but particularly before and after a cycle ride.

Cycling is not a weight-bearing sport and joints are not subjected to wear and tear in the way that veteran runners' joints can be. However, it still makes sense to take care of them. Supplements containing omega-3 fatty acids may be particularly useful for those who are not keen on eating oily fish like salmon, mackerel, herring, sardines and trout. Non-fishy sources include eggs laid by hens fed diets rich in omega-3, walnuts and pumpkin seeds, as well as linseed, rapeseed, soybean, flax seed and their oils.

Masters will have to pay particular attention to fluid intake as the sensation of thirst, not a good indicator of dehydration at any age, becomes reduced with age. To make matters worse, the sweat response to exercise also reduces with age. Adaptation by the kidneys to altered fluid and electrolyte levels and blood flow responses

'Age is not a barrier to performance, only an inconvenience.'

can also all impair thermoregulation in older cyclists. There are no specific fluid recommendations for this age group but certainly general recommendations should be applied vigorously, particularly for those cycling for long periods in the heat. These include hydrating well before training and races, starting to drink before the thirst mechanism kicks in, maintaining a steady, regular fluid intake while out cycling and continuing to drink after cycling until total hydration status has been restored. If there is a choice, veteran cyclists should avoid cycling at the hottest times of the day and keep in the shade as much as possible. Wearing light-coloured clothing and a hat can help reduce the risk of heat stress. Signs of heat stress include muscle cramps, cool dry skin, faster pulse, sickness, thirst and overwhelming tiredness.

Vegetarians

There are six types of vegetarianism, each having a clearly defined list of acceptable foods. Semi- or demi-vegetarians do not eat red meat, though they do eat poultry, game, fish, dairy foods and eggs. This should not present any nutritional problems, though care must be taken to include enough iron. Pesco-vegetarians do not eat meat, poultry or game, though they do eat fish, dairy foods and eggs. Possible nutrients lacking in the diet could be iron and zinc. Lacto-ovo-vegetarians eat dairy foods and eggs but they do not eat meat, poultry, game or fish. They also do not eat gelatine or rennet. Again, iron and zinc are the key nutrients that could be lacking in the diet. The essential fatty acids may also be lacking as lean meat is a good source of omega-6 fatty acids and oily fish a good source of omega-3 fatty acids. Lacto-vegetarians do eat dairy foods, though again no eggs or animal meat; however, the diet could still be lacking in iron, zinc and essential fatty acids. Eggs are the only animal products that ovo-vegetarians eat, and great care must be taken in food choices if recommended intakes of iron, zinc and essential fatty acids are to be adequate. Vegans do not eat any animal products and their diet is made up solely of plant-based foods such as cereals, fruit, vegetables, nuts and seeds. If overall food intake meets energy requirements, protein requirements will also be met. However, the diet must contain plenty of variety of cereals, pulses and green vegetables to ensure all the amino acids are accounted for in the diet on a daily basis. Other nutrients that may also be lacking are vitamin B_{12}, iron, zinc, calcium, essential fatty acids and vitamin B_2. Vegetarian diets tend to be made up of a lot of complex carbohydrate-rich foods, which can make the overall diet quite bulky. This particularly applies to vegan diets. The high-fibre foods that often make up a vegan diet have a reduced amount of metabolizable energy, which could make it harder for a vegan cyclist to meet their energy requirements.

Useful vegetarian sources of nutrients

(Items in brackets will not be suitable for all types of vegetarianism)

Protein: beans, peas, lentils, quorn, textured vegetable protein, tofu, soya, soya milk, quinoa, nuts, seeds, cereals and cereal products (milk and dairy products)

Iron: wholegrain cereals, fortified breakfast cereals, beans, peas, lentils, dark green leafy vegetables, dried fruit, nuts and seeds (shellfish and egg yolks)

Zinc: wholegrain cereals, bread, beans, peas, lentils, nuts and seeds (shellfish, eggs, milk and dairy products)

Calcium: soya milk and soya products fortified with calcium, fortified tofu, sesame seeds and tahini paste, dark green leafy vegetables, oranges, almonds, brazil nuts, peanuts and peanut butter, beans, peas and lentils, white flour and bread which is fortified, hard water (milk and dairy products and canned fish – the bones must be eaten)

Vitamin B$_{12}$: fortified foods including breakfast cereals, yeast extracts, fermented soya foods such as miso (a bean paste/sauce) and tempeh or soya bean cake, supplements (eggs, milk and dairy products)

Coping with Christmas (and holidays)

Christmas is a festive time, and a lot of the fun centres around food and alcohol. Traditional Christmas food tends to be high in fat and it can become all too easy to increase overall energy intake to higher levels than normal. At the same time energy expenditure may be lower as other commitments take over, so that cycling has to take a back seat. There are many pitfalls around Christmas, the main one being a tendency to eat more than usual. There are more temptations to snack, with nuts, chocolates and other nibbles around. Meal patterns can also change, with a tendency to eat more 'big' meals. Instead of a small midday meal and a larger meal in the evening, suddenly it is two big meals. Foods with higher fat content will probably figure more, too. Christmas pudding, mince pies, roast potatoes, stuffings, sauces and chocolates all tend to be high-fat foods. Family commitments may mean that opportunities to go out for a long cycle ride are limited.

Festive season damage limitation plan

- Keep to the usual breakfast – avoid large fry-ups.
- Maintain a regular eating pattern and avoid snacking between meals if possible. Snack on fruit not mince pies!
- Say 'no' to second helpings of high-fat/high-sugar items.
- Avoid skin from poultry meat.
- Dark meat contains more iron and zinc than white meat.
- Make sauces with skimmed milk.
- Avoid cream (or at least keep it to a minimum).
- Have jacket potatoes or boiled new potatoes instead of roast potatoes.
- Pass on the bacon rolls.
- Fill the plate with turkey, potatoes and lots of vegetables.
- Have fresh fruit salad on Christmas Day and save the mince pies for Boxing Day.
- At a suitable time after the meal (unless it is an evening meal) get out on your bike.

Going away on a non-active holiday can also be a time of over-eating, as well as increased alcohol intake. Much of the Christmas advice could help in enjoying the holiday without coming back feeling that fitness levels have dropped and the scales are registering a weight increase. Keeping to a cereal-based breakfast, a regular meal pattern, choosing wisely from menus and being reasonably careful where alcohol is concerned are probably the key pieces of advice to adhere to.

Case Study 6: Chris (the author's husband)

Trip to Paris (as best I can remember)

We started at 7.30am from Twickenham stadium. I cannot remember if I had breakfast. I assume that I did and that it was under your instruction as I followed your instructions to the letter and when I recalled what we ate during the trip on my return, I seem to remember that you approved.

I had Lucozade Sport-powered drinks in sachets. I carried two water bottles with me and drank all the way. Every time we stopped, which was after about two hours, for lunch and then at the port to cross the Channel at 3.30pm, we stoked up on sandwiches, nuts and bananas. I had some energy bars with me too. Sandwiches contained meat, cheese or tuna – I chose tuna. In the evening when we got to where we were staying there was no supper because it was very late. We had had snacks on the ferry going over but that was the usual food they sell on the boats. I had a very nice French sandwich. Cannot remember what it was though. Breakfast was 'continental' and I had cereal, bagel, coffee, fruit juice and fruit. I still had some energy bars left.

On our way to Paris we had stops mid-morning and for lunch at about 1.00pm. It had been an early start, 7.30am. It was very cold and misty and I was wearing the wrong attire. We soon warmed up, after about 1 hour 30 minutes. It was then a very hot day and I drank constantly on the powdered sachets.

We arrived at the hotel we were staying in at about 5.30pm – about 90km from Paris. For the evening meal we had a lot of fruit and pasta with mince (variations of). I had one beer.

Not such an early start in the morning, about 8.30am. Continental breakfast with bananas. Still had energy bars and sachets of sports drink. We stopped twice on our way into Paris, at about 11.00am and then at 1.30pm. Lots of nuts and fruit available. Cannot remember if any sandwiches. Arrived in Paris at about 4.00pm. Then lots of waiting about. I finished the energy bars and my drinks.

Arrived at hotel about 6.00pm. We went out to the formal dinner which was pasta and mince or variations. I think fish was on the menu.

I had done a lot of training and was

used to eating bananas and energy bars. The powdered sachets were great because it saved space and there was always water. When cycling to Paris I used the bottled water that they supplied in copious quantities to dilute the powder.

When training there was never a shortage of water on the way and apart from that I always carried at least three water bottles and topped them up every chance I got. The last training run I did was 108 miles and I stuck to everything you had told me with regard to what went in my mouth.

When talking to other cyclists on the route I felt that my input via the mouth was on a par if not better than theirs. They had not had much preparation food/drink wise. We had lots of discussions and I seem to recall expressing your views to the organizers, who were not so clued up as I was. I say that because even with my limited memory I said enough to persuade them that what I had to say made sense.

During training and the ride itself I followed what you had said religiously, minus the one beer. I never felt that I was over-thirsty/hungry at any time. Nor did I feel full at any time. I felt tired after each day but that was down to the mileage. I was cracking in the miles during training and I am glad I did. Despite advice/comments from the organizers I did not change my intake when on the ride from what I did in training.

I seem to recall that at the stopping points they encouraged the cyclists to fill up (fill up being the operative word) on all that was available, and there was a lot available. It was as though you filled up the tank and hoped that it would last to the next garage (stop). I ate what I felt was sufficient but had rationed out my energy bars so that I could nibble on them during the ride. I ate one about every 30 miles. I would eat it in stages, say over a 5-mile stretch. I also rationed out my two water bottles so that they would last each stage, which was about 20–25 miles. I had got good practice during my training.

Overall I enjoyed the ride and the training and felt that I was very prepared for it. I would have preferred to have done it on a road bike rather than a hybrid. My bum hurt for quite a while after.

CHAPTER 9

INJURIES AND ILLNESSES

Nutrition plays a key part in helping to keep a cyclist fit and healthy, and should he or she succumb to an illness, it can also help to reduce the number of days of inactivity. Similarly a cyclist who is unlucky enough to pick up an injury while cycling (or even when not cycling) may well recover more quickly and be back on their bike sooner if they pay more attention than usual to what they eat and drink during the recovery period. Protein, vitamins and minerals are key nutrients during these times and if the diet contains an insufficient amount of any of them, the recovery from illness or injury may be slowed significantly. While ensuring adequate nutrition to aid recovery, a reduction in overall energy intake will almost certainly be needed if it is going to be some time before cycling, or any other energy-demanding activity, can be resumed. If no attempt is made to reduce food intake to match the reduction in physical activity, body fat levels will increase at the same time that muscle mass decreases. However, although the amount of food will need some adjustment, the quality of the diet should not be compromised as a poor diet will slow the recovery process. One very simple way to achieve a reduction in

overall food intake is just to use a smaller plate or bowl than usual. However, care must be taken to avoid reducing food intake too much as this could slow the time it takes to recover completely. Carbohydrate requirements will be lower during the period of inactivity but protein intake should not change. Care should also be taken not to increase fat or alcohol intake. It is not a wise move to seek solace from the bottle!

Broken bones (fractures)

The key is to balance the need to reduce energy intake, because of the lower energy requirements while unable to train, with ensuring that adequate intakes of nutrients essential for the healing process are achieved. The emphasis on the diet is therefore more about quality than quantity. The nutrients essential to help ensure that recovery is as complete and speedy as possible are protein, calcium, iron, zinc and vitamin C. The major nutrient involved in bone growth and maintenance of healthy bone is calcium and it is therefore vital that the diet contains plenty of this mineral. Milk is an excellent source of calcium, and there are various ways in which it can be incorporated in the daily diet, such as milk puddings, custard and sauces. For cyclists who cannot drink milk (not even if it is flavoured), an effort should be made to include it in the diet by using it in custard or cheese sauce, or making porridge with milk rather than water. A bowl of dairy ice-cream will also provide useful amounts of calcium. For cyclists unable to tolerate milk, a soya milk fortified with calcium provides a good alternative.

Muscular injuries

Injury to a muscle results in swelling and soreness because of an increase in free radicals. These unstable, potentially harmful compounds are produced during chemical reactions in the body that can damage healthy body cells. Antioxidants help to stabilize these free radicals and prevent any damage they might cause. An increase in dietary intake of antioxidants can therefore only be of benefit to cyclists. This can easily be achieved by including plenty of fruit and vegetables in the daily diet. Varying the colour of the fruit and vegetables eaten will ensure the consumption of an even wider range of antioxidants. However, a cyclist who eats only a small selection of fruit and vegetables on a weekly basis is unlikely to obtain the maximum benefit. Having orange juice every day with breakfast is a simple way to ensure a regular intake of vitamin C, a particularly powerful antioxidant. There is further nutritional benefit to consuming cereal and orange juice at the same meal. Most packet breakfast cereals have iron added to them by the manufacturer, and consuming orange juice at the same time as the cereal helps the body to absorb the iron more efficiently. The general healthy eating message to eat five portions of fruit and vegetables a day is partly based on their powerful antioxidant properties. Between them, fruits and vegetables contain hundreds of different antioxidants, particularly the more brightly coloured fruits and vegetables, and a multivitamin and mineral

Oranges are a good source of vitamin C, a powerful antioxidant.

supplement is simply no substitute for including as many fruits and vegetables as possible in the diet.

Muscle damage leads to a breakdown of muscle protein but this does not mean that an injured cyclist needs to reach straightaway for a protein supplement. Including any good-quality protein-rich foods at every meal should be all that is needed to meet requirements. Good sources of animal protein are milk and milk products, yoghurt, eggs, lean meat, chicken, white fish and oily fish. Vegetarian sources of protein are quorn, tofu, nuts and seeds. Many foods eaten for their carbohydrate content also supply protein, but in much smaller quantities. Foods rich in zinc, such as lean meat, can help in wound healing. Oysters and clams are particularly good sources of zinc, although they are probably not included in many people's diets on anything other than rare and special occasions. For vegetarians, dairy products and eggs are the best sources of well-absorbed zinc.

Muscle cramp

Cramp can last from seconds to minutes and it commonly occurs in the calf, thigh and hip muscles after or during strenuous exercise. The *Oxford Dictionary of Sports Science and Medicine* describes cramp as 'A sudden, uncoordinated, prolonged spasm or tetanic contraction of a muscle, causing it to become taut and painful.'

Practical ways to help avoid cramping

- Drink plenty of fluids during cycling to maintain a good hydration status.
- Consider using a sports drink (commercial or home-made) for the sodium (salt) content. Look out for any specially formulated drinks aimed at 'crampers'.
- Do the sweat test in different situations (weathers, type of cycling session) to give an idea of potential losses and therefore fluid requirements.
- Add salt to meals, particularly during hot or humid weather when sweat losses will be higher.
- Include plenty of fruit and vegetables in the daily diet.
- Ensure a good intake of carbohydrate at all meals.
- Refuel with carbohydrate-rich foods and fluids after all training rides and races.
- Have a warm-up routine and stretch before all cycling and other sessions such as weights, and do a similar cool-down afterwards.
- Make sure that cycling kit and footwear is comfortable and not restricting in any way.
- Stretch before bed if night cramps are a problem.
- Remember that recovery after a hard session takes longer than after an easy one.

It is as if the muscle has temporarily forgotten how to relax.

Several causes of cramping have been suggested, including muscle damage, dehydration, an imbalance of electrolytes, low blood sugar levels, irritability of spinal cord neurones (highly specialized cells that generate and conduct nerve impulses) and ischaemia of the muscle. Ischaemia (another *Dictionary* definition) is 'a local and temporary deficiency of the blood supply to tissues, chiefly due to constriction of blood vessels'. Cramps seem to occur more often when muscles are tired, such as at the end of a hard cycle ride or when a cyclist increases their training schedule, cycling longer, harder or more often. All cyclists should allow themselves plenty of rest and recovery time between cycle rides, but especially after hard ones. They should also always do pre-cycling stretching, paying special attention to the muscles prone to cramping, and not start off cycling too quickly. The type of fluid drunk on cycle rides can play an important part in helping a cyclist who is prone to cramping. If cramping does occur, stretching, massaging the cramping muscle and drinking a sports drink should all help to alleviate the cramp – and the pain.

The stitch – or exercise-related transient abdominal pains (ETAP)

Soccer and rugby players, swimmers, horse-riders, runners, aerobic participants and even motorcyclists all suffer from side stitches. A popular view is that stitches happen when sportsmen and women

Ways to avoid the stitch

- Allow between two and four hours after a heavy meal before cycling.
- Stitch-prone cyclists should avoid food and fluid for two hours before any exercise and certainly if cycling on bumpy or uneven roads or terrain.
- Avoid high-fat foods as they take longer to digest than other foods.
- Always start cycling well hydrated and maintain hydration during the ride.
- Avoid hypertonic drinks such as fruit juices, soft drinks and hypertonic energy drinks before and during cycling. (These drinks slow the rate of gastric emptying and could cause distention, increasing the risk of getting a stitch.)
- Drink regular amounts of isotonic or hypotonic sports drinks or water.
- Increase training load gradually, both duration and intensity.
- Learn to relax! Stitches occur more often in tense cyclists. Breathe deeply, making sure the stomach is pushing out with the intake of air. Keep breathing like this until the diaphragm feels loose and free.

exercise strenuously too soon after eating or drinking. However, competitive cyclists have a low incidence of getting a stitch, even though they often exercise very intensively soon after consuming large amounts of food and fluid. Cross-country skiers take on board large amounts of food and fluid before setting off on long-distance treks and yet they seem relatively immune to getting a stitch too. Both men and women get stitches but it seems to affect younger rather than older athletes.

The stitch is a pain in the abdomen area, usually to one side. A bad stitch can feel like a sharp or stabbing pain, a moderate stitch is more like a cramp or ache. For cyclists who do suffer from stitches there are a few practical things to try (see tint box).

Common causes of gastro-intestinal problems

Many gastro-intestinal problems are directly related to exercise. This is because during exercise many bodily functions change in some way – speeding up in some cases, slowing down in others. Stomach emptying slows down, which can lead to regurgitation of the stomach contents back into the mouth. Increased intra-abdominal pressure, through the position of the cyclist, can also lead to gastro-oesophageal reflux. Stomach acid secretions decrease and digested food moves slowly through the small intestine but it moves much more quickly in the large intestine. As blood flow is directed more to the exercising muscles, blood flow to the gastro-intestinal tract can be reduced by as much as 80 per cent. Such problems can intensify as the level of exertion increases or as a cyclist becomes more and more dehydrated. This can cause a vicious circle to develop as the body needs fluids and yet is less able to

utilize them. Cyclists who suffer from gastro-reflux but also train in the evening and then refuel before going to bed may need to make some changes to minimize the effects of the gastro-reflux. If training must take place in the evening, a cyclist should aim to drink a sports drink (with approximately 6 per cent carbohydrate) as a means of rehydrating and refuelling after the session. It is well documented that certain foods are known to aggravate the symptoms, including those with a high-fat content, spicy foods, caffeine-containing drinks, citrus drinks and some smoothies. The cyclist will need to adopt a 'trial and error' exercise to find out what can and cannot be tolerated after an evening training session that finishes relatively close to bedtime. Perhaps the use of two firm plumped-up pillows might prove to be the best solution.

Drinking inappropriate fluids while cycling can be another cause of gastro-intestinal problems. The merits of isotonic sports drinks have been explained in some detail in Chapter 4 but cyclists might still be tempted to try a hypertonic drink. These have a greater concentration of carbohydrate, which may sound very positive but in fact the opposite is true. Because of the amount of carbohydrate present, hypertonic drinks contain more molecules (think of them as particles or 'things') than occur in body fluids and this actually slows down stomach emptying. As a result the replacement of fluids is not nearly so effective. The more concentrated the drink, the slower the process of digestion and absorption, which is the exact opposite of what is needed if fluid is being lost at a faster rate through sweating. A further reason to be cautious about using hypertonic drinks is the increased risk of stomach cramps – a particularly uncomfortable sensation in the gut. Perhaps the worst scenario of all is the potential risk of embarrassing diarrhoea while cycling. Foods high in fat, protein and/or dietary fibre can cause problems too, as can caffeine and alcohol. Nerves alone can lead to poor food intake prior to a race, and for some riders even a very small intake can result in a potentially awkward gut situation.

Overcoming or minimizing gastro-intestinal problems

The incidence of gastro-intestinal problems varies greatly, though female cyclists seem to be more susceptible than their male counterparts. Females tend to be more prone to gastro-intestinal problems during menstruation, and younger female athletes are more prone than older ones. This is probably due to lack of experience and poor dietary choices amongst the younger cyclists. However, overall the frequency of gastro-intestinal problems is considerably less in cycling compared to running.

A cyclist should never do something in a race that has not been tried and tested in training. It is therefore important to experiment with different sports drinks and foods such as cereal bars, sports bars and bananas to find what appeals, is suitable nutritionally and – just as importantly – travels well. Ripe bananas, for example, may not travel too well but 'banana guards' may be a solution (bananaguards.co.uk or lakeland.co.uk). Cyclists who make up their own sports drinks should be meticulous about getting the concentration correct every time. Having a hydration plan that has been tried and tested in training will go a long way to ensuring that gastro-intestinal problems are minimized or avoided completely in competition. Equally an 'eating' plan should be in place incorporating familiar foods, timings and portions.

Cyclists prone to exercise-related gastro-intestinal problems on race days should avoid or restrict their intake of high-fibre foods and certainly should not eat anything they are not used to eating. There is a popular maxim among sportsmen and women that one should never do something in competition that has not been tried and tested in training – something that very much applies to food and fluid consumption.

Food safety

One of the commonest causes of food poisoning in the home is poor handling and storage of food (*see* Appendix 1 – Food suitable for storage in a cupboard, fridge or freezer). A lack of understanding

Ten tips to keep food safe (Food Standards Agency)

- Put away chilled and frozen food in the fridge or freezer as soon as possible.
- Prepare and store raw and cooked food separately.
- Keep the coldest part of the fridge at 0–5°C.
- Check and keep to 'use by' dates.
- Keep pets away from food, dishes and worktops.
- Wash hands thoroughly before preparing food.
- Keep the kitchen clean.
- Vulnerable groups should avoid raw or partially cooked eggs and dishes containing them.
- Make sure food is fully cooked.
- Keep hot food hot and cold food cold.

of information on food labels may also play a part. 'Sell by' and 'Display by' dates are used in shops so that staff know when to remove food items from the shelves. It is not against the law to sell food after this date, but food items that have passed their 'Use by' date must not be sold as they may not be safe to eat. 'Use by' dates are found on the labels of foods that can go off quickly, such as milk, soft cheese, ready-prepared salads and smoked fish. Such food items may look and smell fine but they can still cause food poisoning. These foods usually require storage in a refrigerator. It is important to follow any instructions on the label, including

'Eat within a week of opening', though the food should never be eaten after the 'use by date', regardless of when it was opened. Foods with a 'Best before' date last much longer and include frozen, dried and canned foods. A shop can continue to sell items past this date and the food will still be safe but it may have lost some flavour or texture. Eggs are an exception: although they carry a 'best before' date, they should not be eaten after this date. This is because eggs can contain salmonella bacteria and they could start to multiply after this date.

The immune system

No cyclist likes to miss a training session through illness, let alone a race, and a healthy immune system is the key to making sure this does not happen, or at least in minimizing the risk of it happening. It is the immune system that helps to repair the body after an injury and protects it against bacteria, viruses and fungi that can cause damage. The immune system is made up of physical barriers such as the skin and tissues in the lungs, nose and digestive system, and chemical barriers such as the maintenance of acidity in the stomach as mentioned in Chapter 2. There are also specialist cells called phagocytes which have the ability to engulf and digest foreign organisms or other particles of cells which could otherwise cause harm to the body. Hard strenuous exercise acts as a stressor, depressing the immune system for a short while, although the immune system usually recovers completely after the body has had an opportunity to rest properly. Recovery might not be so quick or complete if a cyclist has a poor diet, has sleep problems or is generally feeling stressed for other reasons, such as work or family issues. In this situation a cyclist could easily succumb to an upper respiratory tract infection.

Cortisol is a stress hormone that is released when hard training sessions are undertaken. Helpfully it helps turn fat and protein into energy sources that the body can then utilize when glucose levels are getting low. However, it has a downside: it limits the effectiveness of phagocytes in destroying invading organisms in the blood and also the effectiveness of the antibody IgA found in saliva. After particularly hard, intense exercise this suppression can last for some hours. Sports drinks are mainly seen as a way of replacing fluid and salt lost through sweating, but research has shown that immune suppression is also reduced if a sports drink is drunk. This is because the intake of carbohydrate from the drink helps to maintain a stable blood glucose level. As a result the body has no need to call on fat and protein to supply fuel and therefore less cortisol is released.

Probiotics are organisms found in the digestive system. They are often called 'friendly' bacteria because they improve the balance of bacteria in the gut by fighting off less friendly bacteria.

Unfortunately the balance of friendly and unfriendly bacteria can be upset quite easily by several factors including stress (not uncommon in sportsmen and women), poor diet, illness and the use of antibiotics. Such an imbalance can cause health problems such as constipation, diarrhoea, gastro-enteritis and thrush, none of which a cyclist would appreciate! Some probiotics have been used for thousands of years, including fermented dairy products and sauerkraut. Cyclists deciding to try a probiotic should choose a reputable brand and check out the relevant website before buying the product. Probiotic bacteria from probiotic drinks and supplements cannot live in the digestive system so they must be consumed on a regular basis. It is also a good idea to follow the instructions on the label! Probiotic bacteria in yoghurts and drinks have a shelf-life of only a few weeks so it is important to observe the 'use by' date. Cyclists who prefer to 'swallow a tablet' should choose a reputable brand, preferably from a chemist's where a pharmacist can give professional advice.

Cures for the common cold

Following this advice may still not be enough to prevent a cold, but there are ways of minimizing its effect. The old wives' tale suggests that a cold lasts nine days: three to come, three to stay and three to go away. For a cyclist who has

Practical ways to reduce the risk of infection

- Ensure adequate rest after training to allow time for adaptations to occur.
- Include one or two rest days each week.
- Eat well and match energy intake to training volume.
- Maintain an adequate intake of carbohydrate. Low muscle glycogen stores can have a negative effect on immunity in response to exercise.
- Eat plenty of fruit and vegetables. Colourful fruits and vegetables tend to have higher levels of antioxidants.
- A broad-spectrum multivitamin and mineral supplement tops up a less than optimal dietary intake.
- Avoid mega-dosing; it can be counter-productive.
- Consider using a probiotic.
- Ensure adequate sleep (around 6–8 hours).
- Sleep quality is important. Keep to a regular pattern. Go to bed and get up at roughly the same time every day.
- Do not share drinks bottles, cutlery or food with anybody, even family. This is one way in which infections are passed on.
- Reduce exposure to bacterial or viral infections by washing hands after using the toilet and before meals.
- Keep hands away from eyes and mouth.
- Cover the nose with a scarf in cold weather when practical. Viruses multiply in the lining of the nose and they breed faster when the cells are cool.
- Avoid dehydration and a dry mouth. Drink regularly during training and races. Saliva contains antibacterial proteins but saliva flow tends to fall during exercise.
- Use a sports drink. The carbohydrate helps maintain immune function. This is particularly important in intense training sessions or in races lasting ninety minutes or more.
- Keep a log of mood, how hard training felt, fatigue and muscle soreness. This can help identify any issues.
- Make some lifestyle changes to include mental relaxation and stress management strategies. Mental stress is closely related to overtraining and an increased risk of upper respiratory tract infections.

caught a cold, this will seem far too long to be out of training. Luckily there are several things that might at the very least help a cyclist feel less grotty, if not actually reduce the number of days off from training. Keeping up fluid intake, eating plenty of fruit and vegetables, and resting and sleeping are the key ones. Symptoms may be eased by taking paracetamol or aspirin, according to the dosage on the label or leaflet. Vitamin C in amounts much greater than the RNI for adults (40mg per day) may help to reduce the severity and number of days of grottiness. Ideally dosing with 500–1,000mg vitamin C should begin as soon as symptoms appear and finish once they have disappeared completely. Sadly, taking

- Avoid contact with anyone with a cold, 'flu or infection, particularly straight after training or racing because of the increased susceptibility to infection in the first few hours after finishing.
- Consider a 'flu injection, particularly for those who are susceptible or at high risk of infection, such as teachers or parents of young children.
- Reduce the intensity and duration of training, or forgo it altogether, if symptoms of illness are present.
- With symptoms of illness above the neck (dry, sore throat, blocked or runny nose, sneezing, slightly swollen glands), undertake light exercise only until the symptoms have disappeared completely, then gradually build up to full training.
- Skip training if symptoms are below the neck (productive cough, general aches and pains, fever, overwhelming tiredness or fatigue, rise in heart rate (+20 per cent). See a GP and ask advice about when to resume training.

such large doses of vitamin C on a regular basis does not prevent the cold in the first place. Taking zinc lozenges as soon as symptoms appear (i.e. in the first twenty-four hours) may help to reduce the severity and length of time the cold hangs around, but dosing should be stopped if there is no improvement after three days. Other treatments that work for some but perhaps not others include dosing with fresh extracts of Echinacea as a tincture (a medicinal extract in a solution of alcohol), eating garlic or chillies, and covering the head with a towel and inhaling steam from a bowl of water to which a few drops of eucalyptus have been added.

Overtraining

The *Oxford Dictionary of Sports Science and Medicine* defines overtraining as 'Training beyond the physiological and psychological capacities of the body to recover during the rest periods.' Typical symptoms include tiredness and yet difficulty sleeping. Fatigue is mental rather than physical, but performance still deteriorates. Specific symptoms include a raised basal metabolic rate, loss of body-weight and a delay in the return of resting pulse rate after exercise. In all training programmes the aim is to train as hard as possible without overtraining, rather like putting a finger near the fire to see if it is hot but not burning it. Symptoms of overtraining include poor sleep so that a cyclist still feels tired on waking. Changes in mood are common and include becoming anxious, more irritable, feeling sad and just not enjoying life as much. Cycling performance invariably takes a dip, even at the same training load. Other markers include weight loss, increase in resting heart rate, fatigue and mood changes, including lack of enthusiasm and depression. These are all symptoms that the cyclist or their family or friends will notice, and medical investigations may reinforce their right to be concerned. These may show a decrease in maximum heart rate, various hormonal changes (notably cortisol, catecholamines, testosterone and insulin), blood chemistry and neurotransmitter changes, including an increase in serotonin levels in the brain, and changes in the immune system. In short-term overtraining syndrome glycogen is depleted and there is a reduction in intracellular stores of water.

Avoiding overtraining

As well as making obvious adjustments to the training programme, ensuring time for recovery after all training sessions but particularly after hard ones, including regular rest days and getting at least eight hours' sleep most nights, diet can also play a part in minimizing the risk of overtraining. Eating a well-balanced, high-carbohydrate diet to ensure maintenance of good glycogen stores and prevention of glycogen depletion is key. Monitoring fluid intake and urinating habits will show if a good hydration status is being maintained. Many cyclists keep training diaries to monitor morning pulse, weekly weight (to check no weight loss has occurred), hours of sleep and quality of sleep. This can provide the wherewithal for self-diagnosis of overtraining, and may be useful information for the GP too!

Iron-deficiency anaemia

Anaemia is a condition in which the amount of haemoglobin in the blood or the number of red blood cells is below the normal range for a healthy population of the same sex and similar age. There are several different types of anaemia but iron-deficiency anaemia is the most common type. Other forms of anaemia are caused by a deficiency of vitamin B_{12} or folate. The main symptoms of anaemia are tiredness and lethargy or lack of energy. Other symptoms include shortness of breath and changes in appearance, including pale skin and dry nails. Treatment usually involves taking iron supplements and ensuring a good dietary intake of iron-rich foods (*see* Chapter 1).

Sports anaemia

This type of anaemia is not related to iron deficiency and a cyclist will have no symptoms; indeed, it is not even regarded as a disease or illness. Many athletes have an increased blood volume but a normal or just slightly increased number of red blood cells. This can give the false impression that the concentration of red blood cells is on the low side. However, the ability to carry oxygen is unchanged – in fact it is probably increased, which is obviously to the cyclist's advantage.

FOOD STORAGE

Foods suitable for storage in a cupboard

Cereal-based foods:
- Breakfast cereals – great snack foods as well as for breakfast
- Pasta – all shapes and sizes. Combine with other store-cupboard ingredients to make salads
- Canned spaghetti and ravioli
- Noodles
- Rice – with sauces, in risottos and salads, savoury rice
- Instant mashed potatoes
- Grains – couscous, bulgur wheat, polenta
- Oat cakes, crispbreads and digestive biscuits – with cheese, honey, jam or Marmite, etc., for snacking
- Cereal bars
- Pizza base – a good standby, add toppings of choice
- Bread sticks, crispbreads, water biscuits, Matzos, etc.

Fruit and vegetables:
- Canned tomatoes (chopped and passata, with or without herbs) – good for sauces and pizza toppings
- Tomato purée
- Canned beans – baked beans, red kidney beans, butter beans, chilli beans, borlotti beans, cannellini beans and chickpeas; add to sauces, salads, soups or mix with vegetables to fill pitta pockets

- Canned sweetcorn – mix with baked beans, use in a salad or serve as a vegetable
- Canned fruit – a good standby if you run out of fresh fruit (buy the fruit canned in natural juices)
- Canned pineapple mixed with low-fat soft cheese makes a healthy filling for jacket potatoes
- Dried fruit – raisins, sultanas, apricots, dried figs and prunes for snacking or adding to breakfast cereals or sandwich fillings

Fish:
- Canned fish – tuna, sardines, salmon, mackerel and pilchards; for sauces, salads, on toast, in pitta bread pockets or as fillings for jacket potatoes

Dairy produce:
- UHT semi-skimmed milk in cartons – a useful standby
- Dried skimmed or semi-skimmed milk – another standby

Drinks:
- Long-life cartons of fruit juice
- Regular or low-calorie squash or high juice drinks
- Regular or low-calorie fizzy drinks
- Tea, coffee, hot chocolate
- Bottled water

Miscellaneous:
- Crunchy or smooth peanut butter
- Marmite, honey, jam and marmalade – for sandwich fillings or toast

- Pasta and stir-fry sauces
- Nuts, fruit and seeds – for snacks, salads and sauces for pasta and rice
- Canned soups – condensed soups can double as sauces
- Canned low-fat milk puddings – quick, healthy and filling pudding
- Canned, cartons or pots of custard
- Instant whips
- Worcestershire sauce, mustards, horseradish sauce, soy sauce, vinegars, mint sauce, chilli powder, curry powder, dried herbs – for flavouring

Foods suitable for storage in a fridge
Cereal-based foods:
- Fresh pasta – e.g. ravioli; cook and top with a little Parmesan cheese

Meat and alternatives:
- Wafer thin ham and smoked turkey – good for sandwich fillings or shredding to add to sauces
- Low-fat liver pâté – for sandwiches
- Eggs
- Quorn and tofu – easy and quick to cook, e.g. in stir-fries, meat-free bolognese, etc.

Dairy produce:
- Semi-skimmed milk
- Yoghurt – low-fat fruit or natural yoghurt
- Fromage frais
- Parmesan cheese – useful for toppings on lots of dishes; has a long shelf-life
- Low-fat soft cheese – for sandwiches, spreading on pitta bread or melting down for sauces
- Cheese
- Low-fat spread, polyunsaturated margarine or butter

Foods suitable for storing in a freezer
Cereal-based foods:
- Spare loaves of bread (can be toasted from frozen), rolls, baps and muffins
- Pitta bread – can be heated up quickly in the toaster or under the grill
- Fruit buns, teacakes and scones. (Thaw out while cycling.)
- Pizzas and pizza bases
- Waffles
- Low-fat Beefeater oven chips

Meat and alternatives:
- Lean mince – for meat sauces and cottage pies; freeze in portions
- Lean cubed meat – for kebabs; freeze in portions
- Low-fat sausages and burgers
- Chicken or turkey fillets – grill or use for kebabs or cooking in a sauce
- Chicken drumsticks
- Chicken nuggets
- Fishfingers and fish cakes
- Fish steaks

Fruit and vegetables:
- All frozen vegetables are nutritionally just as good as fresh, if cooked properly

Dairy produce:
- Ice cream
- Grated cheese

UNDERSTANDING FOOD LABELS

Sell by (display by) dates

These are used by some shops to help staff know when they need to take food products off the shelves. It is not against the law to sell food after this date. However, shops must not sell foods that are past their 'use by' date.

Use by dates

Shops must not sell foods that are past their 'use by' date because they might not be safe to eat. 'Use by' dates are used on foods that could go off quickly, such as milk, soft cheese, prepared salads and smoked fish. Even if it looks and smells fine, using it after this date could put health at risk and cause food poisoning. It is important to follow storage instructions given on labels, otherwise the shelf-life of the food could be even shorter than the 'use by' date. Usually food with a 'use by' label needs to be kept in the fridge.

Some food labels also give instructions such as 'Eat within a week of opening' and it is important to comply. But if the 'use by' date is tomorrow, then you must use the food by the end of tomorrow, even if the label says 'Eat within a week of opening' and you have only opened the food today.

Best before dates

These are used on foods that last longer, such as frozen, dried or canned foods. Shops are allowed to sell foods after their 'best before' date and they will probably be safe to eat. However, remember that if you eat these foods after their 'best before' date, they might not be as nice to eat as they were before that date. For instance, they might have started to lose their flavour or texture.

Until recently the one food that should not be eaten after the 'best before' date was eggs. This was because eggs can contain salmonella bacteria, which could start to multiply after this date. However, the Food Standards Agency (FSA) has now said: 'If salmonella is present in eggs it could multiply to high levels and cause food poisoning. But salmonella contamination levels in UK-produced eggs are low, and salmonella is killed by thorough cooking. This is why the advice is now that eggs can be eaten after their "best before" date, as long as they are cooked thoroughly until both yolk and white are solid, or if they are used in dishes where they will be fully cooked, such as a cake.'

FOOD SAFETY

Improper handling and storage of food and leftovers is one of the most common causes of food poisoning in the home. Training schedules and races can be seriously disrupted by a bout of food poisoning, which can spread if cyclists share a house together. Here are a few simple guidelines to help avoid an upset tummy.

Storing food

- Raw meat and poultry must not come into contact with cooked or ready-to-eat food. Drips from raw food must not fall on other food, including food in the salad drawer at the bottom of the fridge.
- Uncooked foods should be on the lowest shelf in the fridge.
- Cooked and uncooked food should never be on the same shelf.
- Left-overs should be cooled quickly in a shallow dish, covered and then put into the fridge or freezer within two hours. Putting hot food into the fridge causes a rise in temperature and encourages condensation and possible contamination of other foods.
- As a general rule leftovers kept in the fridge should be eaten within two days.
- Hot foods should be kept hot and cold foods cold and not just left lying around.
- Cooked food should only be reheated once, whether cooked in the kitchen or bought as a cook-chill product. Any leftovers after reheating must be thrown away.

- Left-over canned food should be emptied into a bowl or plastic container (not left in the can), covered and stored in the fridge.

Handling and preparing food

- Hands must be clean when handling food and washed between handling raw foods and cooked or ready-to-eat foods.
- Knives and other kitchen utensils should also be washed between handling raw and cooked foods.
- Working surfaces should be washed frequently and thoroughly.
- Particular attention should be paid to washing chopping boards.
- Cooked or ready-to-eat food should not be placed on a surface that has just had raw food on it.
- Vegetables, salads and fruits should be washed in clean, cold running water.
- If using dried beans, including red kidney beans, the beans must be soaked in water for up to twelve hours (or overnight), the water thrown away and the beans then boiled briskly in fresh water for at least ten minutes to destroy the toxins in the raw beans. Canned beans can be used straight from the can as the canning process destroys the toxins.

Thawing and cooking food

- Thawing and cooking instructions on frozen foods should be read and followed carefully. Meat and poultry must be completely thawed before cooking.
- After thawing frozen poultry there should be no ice particles and the flesh should be soft and pliable.
- Food should be cooked well, instructions on the pack should be followed and when food is reheated it should be heated until piping hot.

What not to eat

- Leftovers of questionable age and safety should never be tasted. If leftovers have been stored for too long, or look or smell peculiar, they must be thrown away.

Personal hygiene

- Hands should be washed after going to the toilet and after handling pets.
- Domestic pets should be kept out of the kitchen if possible but certainly away from food, dishes and worktops.

Food Standards Agency ten top tips to keep food safe

- Put away chilled and frozen food in the fridge or freezer as soon as you can.
- Prepare and store raw and cooked food separately.
- Keep the coldest part of the fridge at 0–5°C.
- Check 'use by' dates.
- Keep pets away from food, dishes and worktops.
- Wash hands thoroughly.
- Keep the kitchen clean.
- Vulnerable groups should avoid raw or partially cooked eggs and dishes containing these.
- Make sure food is fully cooked.
- Keep hot food hot and cold food cold.

MEAL IDEAS

Breakfast

- Cereals, any variety, including porridge
- Fruit – any but especially bananas and dried fruit
- Toast, rolls, English muffins, bagels, crumpets, scotch pancakes, currant buns
- Low-fat spread, butter or margarine
- Jam, honey, marmalade, peanut butter, golden syrup, maple syrup, Marmite or Vegemite
- Low-fat soft cheese
- Fruit juice
- Milk, yoghurt, milk shakes, smoothies
- Tea, coffee, hot chocolate, squash, water
- Grilled tomatoes
- Poached mushrooms
- Baked beans
- Lean grilled bacon
- Boiled, scrambled or poached eggs
- Omelettes
- Fishfingers
- Potato cakes
- Cold meats and cheese
- Pancakes

Quick meals and snacks

- Baked beans or spaghetti in tomato sauce on toast or pitta bread (add grated cheese for extra protein)
- Lentil, thick vegetable or minestrone soups with bread, toast or pitta bread
- Toasted muffins with low-fat soft cheese
- Pitta bread with humus
- Jacket potato (cooked in the microwave) with baked beans or tuna and sweetcorn
- 'Halfway pizza' – warm pitta bread under the grill, spread with tomato sauce (not ketchup), sprinkle with canned, drained sweetcorn, top with grated cheese and heat under the grill until the cheese melts
- Omelettes filled with cheese, cooked frozen vegetables, canned sweetcorn and tuna, cooked chicken or ham and eaten with chunks of bread
- Scrambled eggs and sweetcorn on toast or muffins
- Pasta with a quick sauce made with chopped onions, canned tomatoes, garlic and herbs. Top with grated cheese, Parmesan cheese or tuna
- Breakfast cereal with milk, chopped banana and extra dried fruit, nuts and seeds
- Sandwiches made with different breads (baguettes, rolls, bagels) and different fillings (turkey and cranberry sauce; ham, cheese and pickle; tuna and sweetcorn; lean bacon, lettuce and tomato; peanut butter and jam)
- Finish with fresh fruit, cereal bar, cake, yoghurt and a drink

Main meals

Cooked mince meals:

- Spaghetti bolognaise made with lean mince, onions, canned chopped tomatoes, tomato purée and herbs

- Chilli con carne, as above but add canned red kidney beans and chilli and serve with boiled rice
- Shepherd's pie/Cottage pie made as for spaghetti bolognaise, top with cooked mashed potato and serve with peas and carrots

Cooked chicken meals:
- Roast chicken with boiled, roast or jacket potatoes and vegetables
- Chicken stir-fry with vegetables and noodles
- Chicken pieces cooked with onions and canned chopped tomatoes and herbs and served with pasta
- Chicken pieces cooked with onions, low-fat soft cheese added just before serving to make a sauce and served with pasta and peas
- Chicken curry with rice (using a ready-made sauce and extra vegetables)

Meat meals:
- Stir-fried lean beef or pork pieces with vegetables; serve with rice or noodles
- Grilled lean meat with mashed or boiled potatoes and vegetables

Fish meals:
- Pasta with tomato sauce and tuna
- Tuna pasta bake
- Grilled fish or fishfingers with mashed potato and vegetables and a bought sauce (e.g. parsley, mushroom or white wine)
- Couscous, salmon pieces and cooked peas all mixed together and served with a bought (or home-made) honey and mustard sauce

Vegetarian meals:
- Vegetable or lentil curry with rice (using a ready-made sauce and extra vegetables)
- Macaroni cheese with grilled tomatoes
- Deep pan pizza with tomatoes, sweetcorn and cheese

Pudding
- Pancakes with golden or maple syrup
- Sponge and custard
- Fruit crumbles and custard
- Milk puddings
- Instant Whips
- Yoghurt and Muller Rice

REFERENCES

Chapter 2

1. Department of Health Dietary Reference Values for Food Energy and Nutrients for the United Kingdom (London: HMSO, 1991), *Report on Health and Social Subjects*, No. 41

Chapter 3

1. K. Tipton (2007). 'Stimulation of net muscle protein synthesis by whey protein ingestion before and after exercise' (*American Journal of Physiology*, 292: E71)
2. S.M. Phillips (2011). 'The science of muscle hypertrophy: making dietary protein count' (*Proceedings of the Nutrition Society*, Vol. 70: Issue 1)

Chapter 4

1. M.N. Sawka, L.M. Burke, J.B. Leiper (2007). 'Position Stand. Exercise and Fluid Replacement' (*Medicine and Science in Sports and Exercise*, Vol. 39: 377–390)
2. M.S. Ganio, L.E. Armstrong (2012). 'Mild dehydration impairs cognitive performance and mood in men' (*British Journal of Nutrition*, Vol. 106: 1533–1543)

Chapter 5

P.R. Below, R. Mora-Rodriguez, J. Gonzalez-Alonso, E.F. Coyle (1995). 'Fluid and carbohydrate ingestion independently improve performance during 1h of intense exercise' (*Medicine and Science in Sports and Exercise*, 27: 200–221)

Chapter 6

1. N.M. Cermak, M.J. Gibala, L.J.C. van Loon (2012). 'Nitrate supplementation's improvement of 10-km time-trial performance in trained cyclists' (*International Journal of Sport Nutrition and Exercise Metabolism*, 22: 64–71)
2. P.M. Christensen, M. Nyberg, J. Bangsbo (2013). 'Influence of nitrate supplementation on VO_2 kinetics and endurance of elite cyclists' (*Scandinavian Journal of Medicine and Science in Sports*, vol. 23, issue 1: e21–e31)

INDEX